LIVING TOGETHER

YOU, YOUR PARTNER AND THE LAW

JILL BOWLER, JACQUI JACKSON
AND EILEEN LOUGHRIDGE

CENTURY
London Sydney Auckland Johannesburg

First published in the UK in 1991 by Century
An imprint of Random Century Group Ltd
20 Vauxhall Bridge Road, London SW1V 2SA

Random Century Group Australia (Pty) Ltd
20 Alfred Street, Milsons Point,
Sydney, NSW 2061, Australia

Random Century New Zealand Ltd,
18 Poland Road, Glenfield,
Auckland 10, New Zealand

Random Century Group South Africa (Pty) Ltd,
PO Box 337, Bergvlei 2012, South Africa

British Library Cataloguing in Publication Data
Bowler, Jill
Living together : You, your partner and the law
1. England. Cohabitation. Law
I. Title II. Jackson, Jacqui III. Loughridge, Eileen
344.20616

ISBN 0–7126–5016–4
ISBN 0–7126–4642–6 (pbk)

Typeset by Tek Art Ltd, Addiscombe, Croydon, Surrey
Printed by Mackays of Chatham PLC, Chatham, Kent

Contents

The law as stated applies only to England and Wales and is correct as at 21 January 1991.

For notes relating to the law in Scotland and the Republic of Ireland, see Appendices on pages 183 and 207.

The law in Northern Ireland will vary in some aspects from that referred to in this book, and readers in Northern Ireland should bear this in mind.

Preface

Living together outside marriage has far more implications than many people realise. As solicitors working in family law we found that we were seeing more and more people whose living together relationships had come to an end. It was only then that they discovered that their rights to money, contents and property were not as they thought they were. This meant that, at times of great emotional stress, they also had to contend with uncertainty about accommodation and finance. Much of this could have been avoided had they had the information to enable them to make the right decisions at the right time. Our aim in writing this book was to provide a practical and informative guide for people living together, or about to, so that they can be aware of their legal rights (or lack of them) and organize their affairs accordingly.

We would like to thank the following people for their contributions, either direct or indirect, to this book.

First, our partner Craig Smith for having the original idea of providing a service for couples living together. Secondly, all our partners in the practice for their encouragement and support. Thirdly, the staff and our colleagues at Brindley Twist Tafft & James and, in particular, Pauline Crowe, Barbara Sheepy and Barbara James who, under great pressure, managed to get the first draft and revisions completed; and also Alison Barnes, Jennifer Elkington and Barbara Seymour, who enabled the many subsequent revisions to be incorporated into one final typescript. Fourthly, to John and Simon for their patience and understanding.

We would also like to thank David Nicholls MA PhD, Writer to HM Signet, and Muriel Walls, BCL and solicitor, who wrote respectively the appendices on Living Together in Scotland and Living Together in the Republic of Ireland.

Jill Bowler, Jacqui Jackson and Eileen Loughridge
Brindley Twist Tafft & James
3 The Quadrant, Coventry CV1 2DY

SECTION ONE:
You, Your Partner and the Law

Introduction

Living together is on the increase. Ignorance about it is rife but, in this case, ignorance is not bliss. Myths and misunderstandings abound. Did you know, for example, that:

> You don't automatically acquire any rights simply by living together.
>
> Walking away from a living together relationship is not necessarily easier than walking away from a marriage.
>
> You do not automatically inherit your partner's property on death.

If you did not know these facts, you are not alone. Many cohabiting couples do not even think about them until it is too late. It is usually only when things have gone wrong that solicitors are brought in to sort out the problems. And yet, a lot of these problems could be avoided if people were more aware of the implications of living together. There are many positive steps that can be taken.

This book sets out the implications, looks at some of the steps you can take, and the consequences if you do not. It is intended to be informative and practical. A book of this type can, of course, only provide general advice, and cannot take account of individual circumstances.

Will the law change?

The law doesn't stand still. It changes as new laws are made and the courts decide cases. This book covers many aspects of the law relating to family relationships and to the ownership of property. But it will continue to develop, and you need to consult your solicitor before taking any of the steps recommended in this book. There is no substitute for such personal advice.

Who lives together?

More people than ever before are choosing to live together rather than marry. Exact figures are difficult to obtain for a number of reasons. For one thing, there are very few surveys that deal specifically with this point. For another, many people are reticent about answering questions concerned with their private lives put to them by a total stranger. They may have other compelling reasons for not wanting to disclose that they are living with someone – they may be married to someone else; they may feel it is immoral to live with someone outside marriage and want to keep it a secret; or they may be claiming social security benefits as a single person. Even those statistics that are available can, therefore, never be accurate. However, *Social Trends* for 1989, published by the Government Statistical Service, showed that between 1979 and 1987 the number of women aged between 18 and 49 who stated that they were living with someone more than doubled. In 1987, 23 per cent of all births in Great Britain were to people who were not married and, of these, 68 per cent were registered by both parents. Of these joint registrations, almost three-quarters gave the same address for the mother and the father. The indications are that the number of stable family relationships outside marriage is increasing.

It seems likely that the majority of people living together will be heterosexual couples in a stable relationship similar to that of husband and wife. However, people also live together in many other situations.

For instance, living together is the only option available to homosexual couples who do not have the right to marry, but who wish to set up home together.

Also, following periods of rapid inflation in property prices, often the only way a person can afford to buy a flat or a house is to buy it with one or more friends. Before the Budget of 1988, full income tax relief on mortgage interest was available to each part-owner, and this encouraged shared ownership. Even though the double relief has now been abolished, high property prices will still mean that shared house-buying is the only option for many people.

Elderly parents finding it difficult to manage on their own may move in with a son or daughter and family, or they might sell their own home and put the money towards a larger house for them all to share, or for an extension to be built.

An adult child might offer financial help, perhaps in

exchange for accommodation, to an elderly parent who has a chance to buy his or her council house.

It is very important to understand that there are no special rules that apply to you if you are living together in any of these ways. This is quite unlike the position of married couples. Marriage and the law relating to marriage affects many aspects of couples' lives – including property rights, children, inheritance on death, and division of assets on divorce. If you are not married, then the mere fact of living together does not give you any special status or protection.

Even if you have lived together as a couple for a long time, for many purposes the law still treats you in the same way as it would if you had no links with each other at all. This may affect you in ways you don't expect. For example, you have no automatic right to inherit from each other on death, and if you have a dispute about property the court will decide on the basis of facts not fairness.

If you are surprised by the above, don't worry; you are not alone. Myths about living together are widespread, and we aim in this book to explode some of the more common ones.

The myths

Myth 1 – Common law marriage

The myth is that such a thing exists at all. There was once such a concept, but it was abolished in England and Wales about 230 years ago. Despite this, the expression is still in everyday use – as are the terms 'common-law husband' or 'common law wife'. More important than the use of these words is the belief of many people that after they have lived together for a certain length of time they have some special status that gives them rights similar to those of married couples. This is quite incorrect.

The law on marriage as it now stands requires certain formalities before two people are legally married. However, this has not always been the case, and a look at the way in which the law has developed will explain the origin of the common law 'myth'.

Up until about the twelfth century, although church marriage was well established, it was also possible for a couple to be accepted as married simply by having sexual intercourse. However, because it was obviously possible to have sexual intercourse without the couple intending marriage, the custom developed that there had first to be an agreement to marry followed by the physical act (known as consummation of the marriage). This was also later modified so that the physical act was not necessary for a valid marriage, although non-consummation might be grounds for annulment.

From the twelfth century onwards the validity of marriage was governed either by the 'common law' or by Church law. For a marriage to be recognized as valid by the Church usually required solemnization by a religious ceremony. However, a common law marriage needed little formality except for a simple declaration of agreement to marry by the parties concerned. One very important element of the agreement was that it had to be intended to take effect immediately. If the words used suggested that the intention was that the parties should be married at some time in the future, the agreement was still binding on both parties, but did not constitute a marriage; rather, it was an 'engagement' to be married. If one of the parties then refused to go through with the marriage ceremony as agreed, this enabled the jilted party to apply to the court for damages for 'breach of promise'. This right to sue survived for a considerable time. Many people will remember reports of such cases in the press because the right to sue for breach of promise was only abolished by Parliament in 1970.

In the eighteenth century, Parliament passed legislation requiring compliance with certain formalities before a couple could be legally married. The most important was called 'Lord Hardwicke's Act'. One of the reasons was to give greater control and certainty over marriage and remove the possibility of people entering into secret marriages. Landed families, in particular, were usually anxious that the eldest son should make a 'suitable marriage' that would further increase the family's wealth and position. Sometimes, though, a son might fall in love with someone of whom his family would not approve. He would enter into a clandestine marriage that would then be kept secret. He might even go through a form of marriage later on with a person of his parents' choice. The effect of this on a society based on inheritance by the eldest legitimate son could be very disturbing. The melodrama of someone turning up unexpectedly and claiming to be the 'true heir' did not just happen in fiction. And when, on several occasions, members of the Royal Family allegedly entered into secret marriages, something had to be done. Among other things, the new laws stipulated the need for witnesses and for the ceremony to be public. Even today, it is necessary for the door of the church or register office to remain unlocked during the ceremony. The effect of the legislation was to abolish common law marriage and also any rights a common law husband or wife may have acquired under that type of marriage.

Under other legal systems, it is possible to marry with less formality. For example, in Scotland a couple can have a marriage by 'cohabitation with habit and repute'. This requires no formal ceremony, but it is difficult to prove and so is fairly rare.

In England and Wales a church ceremony has been necessary since 1753, and the alternative of a civil ceremony has been possible since 1836. Nothing else will do.

There seems to be no real reason why people continue to believe that common law marriages still exist, other than that couples still refer to each other as 'common law husband' and 'common law wife', and also that the term is constantly used in the media.

This is reinforced by the fact that the state recognizes the existence of living together relationships for certain limited purposes. Many people will have come across this already in connection with social security benefits, where cohabitees are treated as living together 'as husband and wife' and will normally be assessed as a single unit. The Legal Aid Board now also takes into account a cohabitee's income and capital when deciding on an applicant's eligibility for legal aid.

As a general rule, however, people do not acquire the rights against each other of a married couple unless they are actually married to each other.

Myth 2 – 'Walking away is easy'

In contrast, for all the people who think that common law marriage exists, there are equally large numbers who believe that 'walking away is easy'. These are the people who think that living together involves no commitment. Some of the categories are as follows:

The party-goers – These are the ones who go to a party and forget to go home.

The drifters – These start by staying over for one or two nights a week. They gradually find that they have more clothes there than at home, and finally decide they might as well move in – after all, it's cheaper.

The conscientious objectors – These decide that marriage is not for them. This is either because they look upon it simply as an irrelevant piece of paper or, alternatively, because they view marriage as involving too much responsibility; they would feel trapped by legal obligations that could be difficult to get out of if things went wrong.

The battle-scarred divorcees – These have been through the traumas of divorce and have vowed never to risk being in that position again.

The common thread is the misconception that if the relationship fails they can simply pack their bags and walk away. This may be true if they have kept their property and finances strictly separate. But people don't. They open joint accounts, buy property, take out joint loans, and buy things for their home. Extricating themselves from that can then be even more complicated than divorce, because there is no special framework to help the court to divide the property fairly.

Myth 3 – Rights in the home

Many people believe that they acquire rights in the home after they have lived together for, say, six months, or some specified period of time. This is not true. The length of time you have lived together makes no difference at all. The acquisition of rights in property between people who are not married depends on various factors. These include their respective financial contributions to the purchase of the property, and their intentions at the time they purchase or make the contributions.

A mother living with the father of her children will have no automatic right to stay in the home with the children until they are grown up if the relationship comes to an end, unless, of course, she is able to show that the property was hers and remains hers because she alone financed its purchase or that she financed part of the purchase and is entitled to a share.

Caring for the home and family, helping to run the business, sacrificing a career: none of these makes any difference to property rights.

Myth 4 – Right to maintenance

Neither partner has a right to claim maintenance from the other partner. This is the position no matter how long a couple have been living together. The effects can seem very unfair, especially where one of the partners, usually the woman, has given up her own job or career to care for the children of the relationship and is then severely disadvantaged in the job market if the relationship breaks down. Not only is her earning potential likely to be very limited as a result, but she will have no rights to financial assistance from her former partner – even for just a short time to tide her over the transitional period while she re-establishes herself, as she could if married. The children of the relationship will, of course, have the right to claim maintenance from either parent.

Myth 5 – Right to provision on death

As part of the myth that by living together you acquire rights, many people believe wrongly that they are automatically entitled to inherit their partner's estate if he or she dies. If you are not married to your partner and he or she dies, you will not have any automatic right to claim any share of his or her property unless he or she has made a will that says so. You may be able to apply to the court for a share in the estate, depending on the individual circumstances, but the last thing you are likely to want in the period following the death is the added stress of finding out that you are not entitled to anything and the strain of deciding if you should make a claim.

If you do make a claim, you will have hanging over you the uncertainty of not knowing the outcome for a long period of time. Imagine how unsettling this would be to your future plans. This can only make things even more distressing for you at a time when you are trying to come to terms with the loss of your partner.

Differences between marriage and living together

There are enormous differences between the legal position of a couple living together and the legal position of a married couple. Not all of them can be dealt with in a book of this nature, but we will describe the most important ones and some of the more interesting and obscure ones.

To start with, getting married requires compliance with certain formalities. Living together involves no such formalities.

Who can you marry/live with?

You can only be married to one person at a time, but you can live with someone else even though you are still married.

You cannot marry someone of the same sex, but there is nothing to stop homosexual couples living together. There is, however, an age limit (at the moment 21) below which it is an offence for male homosexuals to commit certain sexual acts.

You cannot have a valid marriage where one of the parties to the marriage has changed sex, say from a man to a woman, and is attempting to marry another man. This is because the law does not recognize the change. But again, there is nothing to prevent the couple living together.

The law prohibits marriage between people related to each

other in certain ways. There are about twenty such types of relationship that prevent the parties marrying, but only four of them will prevent the parties living together as 'husband and wife' in a sexual relationship. Indeed, people living together who are related in one of those four ways could face criminal prosecution for incest. Those relationships are grandfather and granddaughter, father and daughter, brother and sister, and son and mother.

Consequences of marrying/living together

Contrary to popular belief, there is no requirement that a wife must adopt her husband's surname, although it is customary for her to do so. It used to be the case that a woman's legal existence was suspended during the marriage or was incorporated and consolidated into that of the husband, so that it was logical for her to adopt her husband's surname. Indeed, there is an old saying that a husband and wife are one person – and that person is the husband. A married woman really had no independent existence during the marriage and, until 1882, could not even own property. Any property she had in her own right before marriage became her husband's property on marriage. That principle no longer applies.

In the case of a couple living together, the partners can use whatever surname or surnames they wish as long as the use of or change of a name is not done with the intention to defraud. If one partner wants to adopt the other's name, the change can be made by a simple document. Strictly speaking, it is not legally necessary to have such a document, but where the partner wishes to register the change of name with a bank, building society or other body, a document will usually be required by that organization.

Marriage places the husband and wife under a duty to live together, so far as circumstances permit. No such duty applies where there is no marriage.

Husbands and wives are under a general duty to support each other financially. This is not the case if you are living together.

Married couples can apply jointly to adopt a child. Unmarried couples cannot make joint applications to adopt.

It is still the case, although there is movement towards change, that a husband cannot be guilty of raping his wife, unless they are separated, but a man can be found guilty of raping a woman he lives with outside marriage.

In criminal proceedings against a married person, his or her spouse can give evidence for the defence and can be compelled to do so if unwilling. A spouse cannot generally be compelled to give evidence for the prosecution. There are exceptions – where the spouse is the victim and the charge involves injury or the threat of injury or certain connected offences, or if the charge involves certain offences against a person aged under 16.

The rules do not apply to persons not married to one another. Each can be called upon to give evidence for the defence or prosecution.

Changes in the law have made married people more independent of one another. For example, the government has now provided for separate taxation of husband and wife as from 1990. People living together as 'husband and wife' have always been treated as independent people for all purposes including taxation, although there are exceptions, some of which we have touched upon in the previous section 'myths'.

Breaking up and dying

There are various ways of formalizing a marriage breakdown, such as divorce, judicial separation or a separation agreement. No formal steps are required to end a living together relationship. When a marriage breaks down, the court has the power to adjust property rights on divorce or judicial separation. This means that the court can redistribute the parties' assets fairly, depending on the particular circumstances. If the parties are not married, the court has no power to adjust their ownership of property, only to decide, on the evidence, who owns what, whether by purchase, gift or contributions.

Where the former matrimonial home is in the sole name of the husband or wife, the other spouse has rights of occupation. The non-owning partner in a living together relationship does not automatically have such rights.

In the same way that married couples do, those living together can make wills to try to ensure as far as possible that the other partner will manage financially when the other dies. But, unlike married couples, living together partners have no automatic right to a share of the other's property if there is no will. If you are still married to someone else, or even if you are divorced, it is possible that your spouse or ex-spouse will be entitled to more of your property on your death than your partner will. If you have left no will, your partner could end up with nothing other than those goods or property that he or she can prove he or she paid for.

Need for advice

If you are living together or thinking about it, you should consider taking legal advice – especially if you are buying property together or if, as is likely, your finances will become mixed.

To avoid problems in the future, it is also important to think about and discuss the financial aspects of your relationship. For instance, you may each make certain assumptions about how the practical side of living together is going to work. You may decide between you that one of you is going to pay the gas, electricity charges, etc. out of his or her bank account and buy the furniture, and that the other will pay the mortgage. You may think that this is a very sensible arrangement and that it doesn't matter who actually pays what, because you both own everything equally. Or do you? If you are both making this assumption, you should have no problem. But what if your partner is making the assumption that, as he or she earns rather more than you and is actually paying the mortgage, he or she owns the whole house: you just own the furniture. Romance may not survive when dealt that sort of blow. If you discuss it now and make sure you are both thinking along the same lines, your romance can continue to blossom in the happy knowledge that there are no nasty surprises in store – for either of you.

All relationships must come to an end eventually, either by

separation or death. Most people would prefer not to think about that and many simply refuse to do so, believing that this would be 'a signal that the relationship might not last', to quote a newspaper article on the subject. One of the people interviewed for the article also said that: 'If you decide to sign a contract, it suggests that failure is in the back of your mind. But if you care about someone, you shouldn't have doubts.' The article went on to mention that that particular couple's home was in the man's sole name and quoted him as saying that he supposed in law his partner would lose out if they separated. His partner might not feel quite as relaxed about that prospect as he evidently did.

We argue strongly that this attitude is about as sensible as saying that you shouldn't take out travel insurance because it means the plane will crash. On the contrary, discussing things openly with each other is positively beneficial. It reduces the scope for misunderstandings and can make your relationship more secure. If these misunderstandings are not sorted out before a living together relationship breaks down, both parties may end up losing out. The partner with no apparent rights in the home or other assets may well feel that it is worth making an application to the court for a share. He or she may get legal aid and may win or lose. Whatever the outcome, the partner who owned the asset will usually also lose out because he or she may pay a high price, emotionally and financially, in fighting the claim. The financial cost will not normally be recoverable in full, even if you win. The emotional cost of such a conflict is incalculable.

On the other hand, if the relationship continues until one

partner dies and you have not sorted things out together beforehand, the one left behind will have to face all the problems alone.

As you will see, it is sensible to talk everything over with your partner and then go together to see a solicitor.

Putting it in writing should provide certainty and security for both of you, and you will know exactly where you stand. You can then forget about the legal niceties of your life together and concentrate on making your relationship work.

Is it too late?

If you are already living together, you will be reassured to know that it is never too late to take the steps recommended in this book. The only essential is that you and your partner agree about what those steps should be.

What are the steps?

The first step is to discuss your relationship, your money, your property, your aims. When you have agreed on these, you should both see a solicitor and discuss your situation with him or her. There may be some instances where your solicitor will consider that, perhaps because the agreement appears to favour one of you more than the other, you should be advised by separate solicitors. Your solicitor will usually want to see the deeds to your property and your existing wills, if any. Having discussed your circumstances with you and considered the documents, your solicitor may well advise you that you need do nothing because your wishes and intentions are adequately expressed in your existing deeds and wills. If this is not the case, he or she is likely to advise you that you need one or more of the following documents:

1 A living together agreement.
2 A deed of trust.
3 A will for each of you.

1 A living together agreement

This can be tailor-made to suit your personal circumstances. It can include terms dealing with almost any matters that are important to you both.

It can deal with how you jointly own property, who pays the bills, who owns the contents, what your liabilities are for debts or loans, what is to happen if you have a child or one of you is unable to work through illness or redundancy, what happens about maintaining children and, finally, what is to happen if you split up: who stays and who goes, and how your possessions are to be divided between you. In other words, it covers property and finance.

We have said the agreement can include almost any terms important to you both, but there are certain areas that you would be well advised to steer clear of. The reason for this is that the court is more likely to enforce an agreement containing only terms dealing with property and finance. Any other terms, for instance, those relating to your personal life together, would probably not be enforced by the court. So it would not be a good idea, for you to include, for instance, terms saying who does what around the house and how much time you spend with each other. More importantly, we would strongly advise against including any terms dealing with sex; these would not only be unenforceable, but the court would almost certainly throw the whole agreement out for being contrary to public policy.

In some states of America, agreements including provisions dealing, for example, with 'quality time' – that is, time committed to enjoying each other's company – have apparently been accepted, but it is unlikely that they would be here. As the whole point of having a living together agreement is to provide certainty, you will see that it is sensible to stick to matters that a court in this country would be likely to enforce; that is, property and finance.

2 A deed of trust

Normally the person whose name is on the title deeds owns the property. However, if you and your partner have decided that you should both be entitled to a share for whatever reason, a deed of trust will be necessary to record this change. This is an additional document that clarifies how you intend to own the property as between yourselves. Another way of dealing with this would be to transfer the title deeds into your joint names, but this may not always be appropriate.

On the other hand, if the title deeds are already in your joint names, but the shares are not clear or you want to change these, a deed of trust is the only way of recording the changes. It declares what proportions of the value each of you is to have, and how those proportions should be calculated.

3 Wills

These are familiar to most people, even if they have never made one themselves. Wills set out what you want to happen on your death – who you want to sort out your financial affairs, who you want your property and belongings to go to, and who you want to look after your children. You will see from Section 4 how important it is for you both to make wills. These can always be changed later if your circumstances change. To sum up, then. When your solicitor has helped you to discuss and clarify exactly what your aims are, the necessary documents can be drawn up quite easily to help you give binding legal effect to your wishes. The result will be a legal framework that can give you both the sense of security you need to have in the background so that you can confidently concentrate on your life together.

SECTION TWO: Living Together

Introduction

This part of the book deals with the main things you need to know when you are intending to live together. Most of it will also apply to you if you are already living with a partner. You needn't worry; it is not too late to take the necessary steps. Thc only essential is that you both agree on what you want.

Different people will choose to sort out the practical side of living together at different times and different stages of their relationship. There are some extremely well-organized people who discuss and agree the financial aspects before moving in together. Others, at the beginning of their relationship, will feel it destroys the romance even to think about money and property, let alone about separating and dying. Or they may think about it, but be reluctant to broach the subject for fear of appearing mercenary. Many are relieved to find that when they do eventually mention it, their partner has been thinking along the same lines. Still others, perhaps after the initial 'honeymoon period' has passed, will realize that not to think about and discuss such things will eventually kill the romance because of the disagreements that are bound to arise from time to time when two people are sharing a home. The first disagreements may be over something as stupid as whose turn it is to pay the milkman or settle the newspaper bill. One of you may have assumed that the other was always going to pay for those things just because they did so for the first few weeks. Your partner may have assumed that you were going to take it in turns – but didn't like to mention it because it would seem mean.

If you have not discussed these minor matters, it is quite likely that you have not discussed the major ones, like who is to pay the mortgage and endowment policy premiums. Or you may have talked about them from a purely practical point of view, but may not have realized that the arrangements you make have legal implications that you had not anticipated.

For instance, you may be buying the home jointly and may have agreed that your partner will pay the mortgage from his or her bank account because it is more convenient that way. Without stating it in so many words to your partner, you may assume that this is a purely practical arrangement that will not affect your share in the home. Your partner, on the other hand, may take the view that paying the mortgage should entitle him or her to a greater share of the proceeds of sale if it is sold.

If the court is called upon to settle a dispute between you about the ownership of the property, it will look at what you both intended at the time. In the example given, if you have not discussed this at all, it may well emerge at the court hearing that your partner's intentions were apparently quite different from yours.

The court will also look at what financial contributions

you have each made, and this could be a problem if you have not made any direct contribution to the purchase of the property, even though you have bought all the furniture, paid the water rates, gas, electricity and telephone bills. You could well end up with just the furniture and no share in the property.

You are likely to end up with nothing at all if you separate. If the property is in your partner's sole name and you had thought that by paying all household bills and buying furniture you would acquire a share in the home, you will be on extremely shaky ground. You are likely to end up with nothing at all if you separate and your ex-partner does not do the decent thing and give you a share.

If potential problem areas like these are not sorted out between you, the misunderstandings will increase and cause romance to fly out of the window. The purpose of this section is to tell you what you need to know about the financial implications of living together, so that you can avoid the problems and make sure that your relationship continues to flourish.

ONE: Your Home

Your home is probably very important to you. Apart from anything else, it is likely to be the largest financial investment you will make. For that reason, you should both ensure that it will be secure for the future. If you decide to live together, you will be going from two homes to one. There might come a time when you feel you would prefer to go your own separate ways. You would again need two homes and would have to make a decision on what to do about your joint home. What happens then will depend substantially on what you do about it at this stage. Taking the right steps now will be rather like taking out an insurance policy. You are pretty sure you will never need to cash it in, but it is comforting to have it there – just in case.

The steps you take will depend on whether you own the property that is your home; or whether you rent it and, if so, what sort of tenancy it is.

Note: If you have a secure tenancy it is worth considering what you are giving up if you move into a home with your partner. A secure tenancy is a valuable thing to have. Will you get something in return for giving that up?

1 Buying

More and more people are now buying their homes, usually with the help of a mortgage. If you have bought or are about to buy, there are important questions that you need to think about. After all, you are acquiring a valuable asset.

(a) *Is your home in joint names?*

If your home is in joint names, both names will be on the title deeds. The deeds will say whether you own as 'joint tenants' or as 'tenants in common'. These are technical terms and have nothing to do with renting or living in tenanted property. In this book we have used the terms 'joint owners' or 'owners in common' rather than the technical terms, because we believe they convey more clearly the different types of ownership.

The distinction between joint owners and owners in common is important, and if you are in doubt as to how you own the property you may want to ask your solicitor to check your deeds. If you have a mortgage, the deeds will have to be obtained from the building society or other lender.

(b) *Do your deeds say that you are joint owners?*

If they do, then technically the law treats you as if you own the whole property between you.

If you subsequently sell, this means that you are almost certainly entitled to half each of the net proceeds of sale.

If one of you dies, the other automatically inherits the whole of the property regardless of what you may have said about it in your will, and regardless of who inherits the rest of your property if you do not leave a will.

You may be quite happy about this, but there may be circumstances in which you would each prefer to retain control over your share so that you can, for example, leave it to your children from a previous relationship. If this is the case, or if you both want to change the size of the shares, you should consider changing so that you own as owners in common.

(c) *Do your deeds say that you are owners in common?*

If you are owners in common, the law treats both of you as if you each owned a share in the value of the property. The deeds may specify the proportions (e.g. one-third to one, and two-thirds to the other) but, if they do not, the shares will probably be equal – although this may be open to argument. You can say in your will who is to have your share when you die. If you don't leave a will, your share will go to whoever is entitled to the rest of your estate. This will not be your partner (unless there are very exceptional circumstances).

If the deeds do specify the shares, you need to decide whether those shares are what you both want. For example, one of you may have contributed more to the value by paying a higher percentage of the mortgage, and you may want to adjust your shares to reflect this.

(d) *If your home is in the sole name of one of you*

There may be several reasons for this. One of you may already have owned the property before the other came on the scene. Or you may have had the property as part of a settlement on divorce. Whatever the reason, you need to decide whether you and your partner are to share the ownership of the property or whether it is to remain the sole property of one of you. If only one of you has contributed to the purchase of the property or its value, then you may both agree it is appropriate to leave it in the sole name and that the other should not have any share in its value. If that is the case, it is much better to make it clear by putting a statement of your joint intentions on paper.

(e) *Have you made a contribution?*

Whether or not your name is on the deeds, you may have made a contribution that increases the value of the home, and you may both feel that this should entitle you to a share in the value, or a bigger share if you are already joint owners. If this is what you want, you should record your intentions in writing because, if you should be unable to agree later on, the court would decide on the basis of what it thought your intentions were at the time of the contribution. A contribution may include payment towards the deposit or mortgage instalments or payment for improvements (but these must increase the value of the home). Only rarely can it include payment of household expenses or physical labour, and then only if it is out of the ordinary. Just doing the decorating or minor repairs will not count.

(f) *Making sure your shares are clear*

If your home is in joint names and you are joint owners, you need take no action unless you want to change this. If you would rather have distinct shares, for example, to leave by will, or if you do not want your shares to be equal, then you need to see your solicitor. He or she will be able to change the way in which you own the property in one of two ways. The first is by preparing a 'memorandum of severance of joint tenancy', which you can both sign, or one of you can sign a 'notice of severance' and serve it on the other. In either case, it simply states that from a certain date you own the property as owners in common and no longer as joint owners.

The second way in which you can change how you own the property is by a deed of trust. This is a document that will be placed with the title deeds as evidence of your shares. If you intend to change the proportions, this is the more appropriate way of doing it.

If the home is in your joint names and you are owners in common, you probably don't need to do anything unless you want to change the shares. If so, you would need the deed of trust as described above.

If the home is in the sole name of one of you and you have decided that you are both entitled to a share because, for instance, you have both contributed, you will need either to transfer the property into joint names to be held either as joint owners or owners in common, or you will have to record your shares in a deed of trust.

In some cases, you may both feel it is right that the other partner should not acquire an interest at all. That too should be recorded in writing to help avoid problems later. As an additional safeguard, it would be wise for both of you to seek independent legal advice before doing this.

Where the title to the property is registered, any change in the way you own the property will need to be notified to the Land Registry.

Family loans and tenancy discounts

You may be fortunate enough to have a family who can lend you part of, or all of, the purchase price of your home. If that is the case, it is advisable to record the loan and the terms of repayment in a mortgage deed that your solicitor can draw up for you. This is especially important for couples living together as you and your family are likely to want to make sure that, if you should separate or if one of you should die, there is no confusion about the loan or its repayment.

It is perhaps more important to consider the position where your family makes a gift of a lump sum towards the purchase of a property. If things go wrong between you, you will probably not want your ex-partner to derive the same benefit as you from your family's gift.

There could also be the situation in which your parents already own a second property, perhaps because they have inherited it, and are willing to let you buy it for less than the market value. It is advisable to think ahead and decide now what effect you want this to have on your shares – that is, whether you both feel that your partner should benefit from your parents' generosity.

Similar considerations apply to the situation where you are buying a council house with the help of a tenancy discount. If the tenancy was in your sole name, then you may agree that the tenancy discount should be treated as a contribution to the purchase price. If you are purchasing in joint names, you may wish to consider holding the property as owners in common to allow your respective shares to reflect your initial contribution. Your solicitor will be able to help you work out the best way of doing this.

Prior ownership

People cannot always neatly arrange their lives so that they are ready to start living together at exactly the same time as they are ready to buy a house. It is quite likely that you will already have bought a home at some stage and that you agree that your partner will come and live with you there. Alternatively, you may both be home-owners and decide that you will sell one home and both live in the other, rather than sell both and start from scratch. You need to consider very carefully the financial implications for both of you. There are many options. Some are listed below, but you or your solicitor may come up with others:

1 You own a property. If you sold it, and paid off the mortgage, any money left over would be what is called the 'equity'. You may feel that the value of the equity at the date your partner moves in should be yours whatever happens. However, you may want to share payment of the mortgage and the value of the property from now on. You might consider transferring the property into joint names, but as owners in common. You could have the property valued as at the date your partner moves in, and the deed of trust could provide that you should have a certain lump sum or a certain percentage before the balance of the eventual proceeds of sale is split between you.

2 You both own properties, but you are going to sell yours and move in to your partner's home. What do you do with your proceeds of sale? You could agree that you use some or all to improve your partner's property or pay off part or all

the mortgage, and in return for this the property is transferred into your joint names – as joint owners or as owners in common in shares calculated to reflect your respective contributions.

3 Alternatively, you both may decide to use those proceeds of sale, or, indeed, your savings, for complete redecoration of your partner's property and to buy some new furniture, or even to have your dream holiday. Although the money has not been used directly for the purchase or improvement of the home, you may both recognize that the lump sum has been used for the benefit of you both, and that this very indirect contribution should give you a share in the property. If this is what you decide, it is vital that the property is transferred into your joint names or your shares recorded in a deed of trust. Obviously, such an exercise is only worth doing if a substantial sum is involved.

Mortgages

The vast majority of people buying their own home will do so with the assistance of a mortgage. Mortgages are available from banks, building societies and other financial institutions, and usually require repayment over a period of twenty to thirty years. If you are in a position to repay over a shorter period, that can be agreed with the lender.

You can make a joint application. Nowadays, the lenders are not concerned about your relationship with each other, or about your not being married. They will want to know about your financial circumstances to satisfy themselves as to your ability to pay. They will also want to have the property valued to ensure that the market value is greater than the amount you wish to borrow. This is in case the day comes when you cannot afford to continue the repayments. The mortgage will enable the lender to apply to the court to repossess the property in order to sell it. You would be evicted and, if at the end of the day there was any money left over, it would be paid to you. This would make it difficult for you to obtain another mortgage.

A reminder: If the mortgage is joint, you will be jointly and severally liable for the debt. This means that each of you is liable for the whole amount, not just half. If your partner disappears, or refuses or is unable to pay, the lender can claim the entire debt from you alone. You can claim a contribution from your partner – if you can find him or her and if the money is available.

You may also take out loans with other lenders, who may include finance companies. They might lend relatively small sums of money, but insist on you signing an additional document which is, in fact, also a mortgage over your property.

Failure to make the payments on any mortgage, whether with a building society or finance company or other lender, is likely to result in you losing your home, as described above.

There are various types of mortgage on offer, and you should consider carefully and take advice as to which is the most suitable for you. The main ones include 'ordinary repayment' and 'endowment linked' mortgages.

An ordinary repayment mortgage means that every month you repay part of the capital sum borrowed plus interest on the loan. At the beginning of the mortgage term the capital element of each instalment is quite small, and you will be paying mostly interest. Gradually, the capital element increases so that the whole of the sum borrowed has been repaid by the end of the term. You can take out a mortgage protection policy to ensure that the mortgage is paid off if one of you dies.

An endowment linked mortgage means that the loan is secured both against the property and against an endowment insurance policy that the borrower(s) take out on their own lives. The benefit of the policy is then assigned to the lender. The repayments to the lender are of interest and not capital, and are therefore lower than with an ordinary repayment mortgage. However, as well as each monthly interest payment to the lender, you also have to pay the endowment policy premiums. The two payments together may amount to more than the single monthly payment under the ordinary repayment system. When the endowment policy matures at the end of the term, the proceeds are used to repay the sum borrowed.

The main advantage of the endowment policy is that it also provides life assurance so that, if one of you dies during the term of the mortgage, the benefits payable under the policy will be paid to the lender to clear the mortgage. The exact terms of the policy should be checked to establish what benefits will be paid and whether on the first death or the second. Although the minimum amount payable on death is guaranteed, the amount payable on maturity is not, and it may be more or less than the amount owed to the lender.

2 Renting

As was mentioned earlier, a secure tenancy is a valuable thing to have. If you are both in rented accommodation, should it be the one without a secure tenancy who should move?

If you decide to rent accommodation together, there are relatively few formalities. You need to decide whether to rent in the sole name of one of you or in your joint names.

If the tenancy is joint, you will each be liable for the whole of the rent. This means that the landlord can demand the rent in full from either one of you and is normally under no obligation to demand half from each of you. So if one of you becomes unemployed and unable to contribute towards the rent, the other will be liable for the full amount. You will, in theory, be able to claim half back from your partner as co-tenant, but this right may be meaningless if the reason for non-contribution in the first place was lack of money.

By the same token, if the tenancy is in the sole name of one of you, that person alone is liable to the landlord, whatever the practical arrangements for payment you and your partner may make between you. Remember that you may need your landlord's permission if the tenancy is in your sole name, and you want your partner to move in with you. Check your tenancy agreement if you have one.

Your right to occupy depends on whether the tenancy is joint or in the sole name of one of you. If the tenancy is joint, both of you are entitled to live there, as long as you are not in breach of the terms of the tenancy agreement. If the tenancy is in the sole name of one of you, only that person has a legal right to live there. Anyone else living there does so by invitation, and that can be withdrawn at any time.

3 Insurance

If you are living together it is particularly important for you to be careful when you take out any sort of insurance cover. This is because you may assume that if you take out a policy it will cover the people, property and risks you want it to cover. Also, you may assume that the insurance company will tell you what it wants to know, and that if it doesn't then that particular piece of information is not important. It is wise not to assume anything. Check that the policy covers what you want it to cover and be sure to tell the insurance company everything that might be relevant. If you do not, you may find you are not covered.

We have already touched on certain types of insurance in relation to mortgages, but you will need other types of insurance as well.

Some of the main points to bear in mind are as follows:

Contents insurance – You will need to read the policy to check whether your partner's possessions are covered if you are the sole policy holder. They may not be. If your partner's children from a previous relationship live with you, check whether their property is covered. If you are not a policy holder, you may be treated by the insurance company merely as a visitor. If so, the policy will probably only cover your personal possessions to a limited extent, for example to the value of £100, and you may lose out if your property is stolen or damaged. Always read your policy and make sure the amount of cover is adequate.

Life assurance – This is slightly more complicated. There was a time when anyone could insure anything, or anyone. In the early stages of the development of the insurance industry it was possible for people to insure the lives of public figures – for example, the Prime Minister. The insurance company would then pay the lump sum ('the sum assured') on the death of the Prime Minister. This was stopped by the Life Assurance Act 1774. This Act and other legislation prevented policies being taken out on another's life or on an event, except where the person taking out the policy could show he or she had an 'insurable interest'.

An insurable interest means that the person taking out the policy must have an interest in the preservation of the thing insured – that is, he must stand to lose financially if the risk insured against occurs. The amount of the benefit payable must be related to the amount of the loss that the person taking out the policy is likely to sustain. For example, if you have a joint mortgage and your partner dies, you will lose financially because you become solely liable for mortgage repayments. Taking out an endowment policy or a mortgage protection policy in those circumstances falls within the rules.

Everyone is regarded as having an interest in his or her own life, and can therefore take out life assurance or can insure against accident or ill health. But to take out a policy on the life of someone else requires an insurable interest that in turn requires some sort of potential financial loss if the person insured dies.

Husbands and wives are deemed to have an insurable interest in each other's lives. People living together are not, and must show an insurable interest. This may not always be possible except for insurance covering specific joint liabilities such as joint mortgages or other debts.

Is there a way round this?

If you wish to make sure your partner is provided for on your death by means of insurance, you can do it in the following ways:

(a) By taking out a policy on your own life and naming your partner as the person entitled to the benefit paid out on your death.

(b) By taking out a policy on your own life so that the benefit will form part of your estate on your death. You would then, of course, have to make a will leaving your estate, or part of it, to your partner, to ensure that he or she did receive the benefit.

(c) By taking out a policy on your own life and providing that the benefit is held in trust for your partner.

(d) By taking out a policy on your own life and assigning the benefit of the policy to your partner.

However, if you choose options (a), (c) or (d), you should remember that you cannot change these later without your partner's co-operation. Even if you stop paying the premiums, the existing value of the policy will still belong to your partner.

So, you must obtain good advice, and check your policy to ensure it covers the people, property and risks you intend that it should. And you must make full disclosure of all relevant information to the insurance company. A contract of insurance is said to be a contract 'of the utmost good faith'. The effect is to require you to disclose anything that might have a bearing on the risk the insurance company is taking. If you do not, the insurance company might refuse to pay out on the policy.

There are many different types of insurance and you should consult a broker or insurance company or other adviser before taking out a policy, so that you can ensure that you have the cover you need.

TWO: Contents and Money

1 Contents

Contents are often a problem. It is surprising that people can spend a long time arguing over contents (whose second-hand value is usually negligible) when they have managed to reach agreement quite quickly and painlessly over the house – which is a far more valuable second-hand item. Unless the contents are valuable because they are antiques, it is never worth undertaking court proceedings unless the home is in dispute as well. It can happen that someone feels so strongly about the return of a particular item, perhaps for sentimental reasons or over a question of principle, that he or she is prepared to go to court over it, but that person must be willing to pay a high price for that sentiment or that principle. It is only rarely worth it.

The basic point to bear in mind is that items given to you personally, or paid for by you out of your own separate money, are yours. Items bought out of joint monies are joint property. It follows that items you brought with you to the joint home are yours, but it also follows that anything you buy with your own money during the period you live together is yours – even if you bought it for your joint use.

Disagreements often arise over 'gifts'. If your partner gave you a washing machine or a microwave for your birthday, is it yours because it was a present to you, or is it your partner's because he or she paid for it? If your parents buy a freezer does it belong to you only or to both of you?

If there are certain things that are important to you – the expensive camera because photography is your hobby, or the computer and associated software and hardware because you need them for your work, or the antique chest of drawers that Aunt Doris left you – it is sensible to discuss this and agree between you, preferably in writing, that these things will belong to you whatever happens.

Personal items are less likely to give rise to disputes, but could do where they are valuable things such as jewellery or a stamp collection. Again, you should discuss this and, if possible, record your decisions in writing.

Items bought on credit or hire purchase will belong to the person whose name is on the agreement. Again, this can cause problems where the item was bought as a gift for your partner. The item may belong to your partner if it was an outright gift, but you remain liable for the repayments – even if you split up. This is the case even where your partner agrees to make the payments. If he or she defaults, the finance company or bank will claim payment from you regardless of the private arrangements between you and your partner, and regardless of whether or not you still have the item in question. The finance company will not normally agree to you assigning the agreement to anyone else, so you should think ahead when taking on any such commitments.

The same points apply to joint agreements. If you take on any such liability, you remain 'jointly and severally' responsible.

This does not just mean that you have to pay your half. It means that the finance company can take proceedings against either or both of you for the whole amount of the debt outstanding. Once the creditor obtains judgement against you both, the company can decide which of you is the most likely to have the money to pay, and will almost certainly enforce judgement against that person – a double blow if you have let your partner have the goods.

2 The car

After your home, your car may be your most expensive purchase. It is likely to be a purchase that is planned and for which you have saved, or for which you have taken on the liability of a loan. It is important that ownership of the car is clear.

Many people believe that the owner is the person whose name is on the registration document (formerly known as the logbook), but this is not necessarily the case. The registration document is not proof of ownership. That document simply records who is the registered keeper of the vehicle. As an example to illustrate the point, consider the vehicle bought on hire purchase. You will not own that vehicle until the final instalment has been paid. Until then, the car belongs to the hire-purchase company, although the registration document may have your name on it. This is because you are the keeper – but not the owner.

If there were to be a dispute about the car at a later date, the court would decide who owns the car by looking at who actually bought it. If you went to the dealer and paid for the car with your own money, then you own the car regardless of whose name is on the registration document.

Confusion can arise where you go to a dealer to purchase a car, but the money was provided by your partner. On the face of it, you own the car because you contracted with the dealer to buy it. But if your partner provided the money, he or she may be entitled to the car unless you can show it was an outright gift to you.

The position is in some ways clearer if you bought the car with some form of credit. If the credit agreement is in your name and you are making the repayments, the car is likely to be yours – again, unless your partner can show the car was intended to be an outright gift to him or her. The differences between ownership of an item and liability for the credit facility used to buy the item are dealt with more fully in the section on credit on p. 49.

3 Bank and building society accounts and other assets

You can arrange your financial affairs in any way you choose and this may include opening a joint bank or building society account for payments and savings. You can also, of course, retain separate accounts if you wish. If you do have a joint account, you should remember that you will both be jointly and severally liable for any overdraft, whoever incurs it. Again, the bank can claim the whole amount from either or both of you.

You will usually be able to choose how you operate the account – either on one signature or both to sign for all withdrawals.

If one of you dies or you separate, it may not be entirely clear how the balance in the account is to be divided. *Joint is not necessarily equal.* If there is no clear agreement, division will depend on how the contributions were made to the account, and that may not result in equal division. You should both be quite clear on your intentions at the beginning, and make sure these are properly recorded in an agreement or a letter to the bank.

The same principles apply to other assets and investments such as stocks and shares.

4 Credit, loans and services

People obtain credit in many ways and from various different sources. It may not have occurred to you, for instance, that you are obtaining credit from your local electricity supplier for the electricity you use (unless you have a slot meter) from the time you use the electricity until the time you pay the bill. The same applies, of course, to gas and telephone services. And in all cases, as far as the person or company giving credit is concerned, the debt is owed by the person whose name is on the account. This has important implications; if your name is on the gas bill then the gas supplier is entitled to collect the debt from you, even though you were not the only one using the gas.

You can arrange between you that, on a practical level, you are each going to pay half the bills. But this will not cut any ice with the gas or electricity suppliers. They are not concerned with private arrangements between you and your partner, but are only really concerned about obtaining payment of the debt. If it becomes necessary to take you to court to recover the debt, it is the person whose name is on the agreement who will be at the wrong end of the county court summons, and the visit from the bailiff if that is the only way of recovering the money. This could happen, for instance, if one of you was made redundant or had an accident and was unable to work. If, having budgeted on the basis of two incomes, there was not enough money to pay all the bills, you could find yourself being sued.

For this reason, you should discuss between you who is to sign the agreements for the electricity and gas supplies and the telephone. Suppliers frequently disregard communications notifying them that the property is in the joint occupation of two people, married or not, and often address their demands to the man only. That can, of course, be useful if you later split up and your name is not on the demand. However, it is usually preferable to make a positive decision about such matters, rather than to leave it to fate and the personal foibles of the operator putting the details on to the computer.

All these accounts can be joint if you ask for them to be joint. If that is what you decide, and if you both sign the agreement with the relevant authority or company, you will both be jointly and severally liable for the debt. Joint and several liability basically means that the creditor can claim the whole amount of the debt from either or both of you. In practice, the creditor will usually sue both and obtain judgement against both, but only enforce the judgement against the one who seems most likely to be able to pay.

If the debt is joint and you have been called upon to pay

the whole amount yourself, you could claim a contribution from your partner if his or her name was on the agreement. If the agreement only had your signature on it and not your partner's, then you will not be able to claim a contribution from him or her.

The above principles also apply to other types of credit, such as bank loans, credit cards, hire purchase, etc.:

Bank loans and overdrafts – If the account is in your sole name, you are solely liable for any overdraft on the account. The same applies to loans, and you are solely liable even if the item purchased with the loan was for your joint use. If the account or loan is in joint names, then your liability for any overdraft is joint and several in relation to the bank, as explained above – that is, the bank can claim the whole debt from either or both of you.

Credit cards and authorized users – Most, if not all, credit cards are in the sole name of one person, although most credit card companies allow the cardholder to nominate 'authorized users'. An authorized user will be given his or her own card with which he or she will be able to make purchases on your account using his or her signature. But bear in mind that you will be liable for payment of any outstanding balance on the account.

Hire-purchase and other credit sale agreements – If only one signature is on the agreement, only that person is liable to the finance or hire-purchase company. If both of you have signed, you are both jointly and severally liable to the company.

Guarantees – Giving a guarantee is not the same as obtaining credit in your name, but it can have similar implications. For instance, if your partner wishes to buy a motorbike, but she wants to buy it on credit, the finance company may not consider she earns enough for the amount she wants to borrow. Alternatively, the company may not feel she is a very good credit risk. If so, they may ask her to get a parent, or even her partner, to be guarantor. If you sign a separate guarantee or if you sign the finance agreement guaranteeing the debt, should your partner default on the repayments, the finance company will claim the money from you to satisfy the debt.

Family loans – These are rather different from other types of loan, partly because there is not usually any written agreement and partly because there is always likely to be some doubt about to whom exactly the family was lending the money. Most people would probably assume that the loan is to both of you because it is made to you at a time when you are happy together and you need funding for some joint project. But the situation might be quite different if you separate. You may still feel that your family made the loan to you jointly; but your ex-partner may not agree and may refuse to contribute towards the repayments. To avoid this sort of problem, it is better to have a written record of such a loan and the basis on which the loan was made – whether to one or both of you, and when and how it is to be repaid.

Remember: Ownership of an item bought on credit and liability for repayment of the credit are not necessarily with the same person. To avoid problems, you should think in advance about which of you would wish to have the item if you separated, and try to ensure that that person is liable for credit repayments.

You should always read the terms and conditions of a loan, credit agreement, etc. before signing it. Some general principles have been set out above, but they are not claimed to be comprehensive.

THREE: Businesses

Nowadays, many people are running small businesses or small companies. This can sometimes be a joint venture with your partner. If you are involved in a business relationship as well as a personal relationship, then obviously it is doubly important that you both consider what would happen to the business if you later separate or if one of you dies; and that you discuss this fully with your solicitor and other financial advisers, preferably when setting up the business. (See Example A.)

Example A

The first thing David and Fiona found out about each other was that they were both mad about old canal boats. So when they started living together they also started making plans. First, they bought a canal boat, then they set up a business running day trips for tourists. This was very popular and soon became very successful. They found a lock-side cottage and bought this together. It was larger than they needed, so they started combining bed and breakfast with the boat trips. They also borrowed capital from the bank and bought a further two boats. This meant employing four other people in the business. Eighteen months after this, Fiona was killed in a motorway pile-up. She had not made a will. Because they had bought the cottage as joint owners, this automatically went to David; but Fiona's half share of the business went under the Intestacy Rules to her parents. They didn't want to know about the business, only how soon they could have their share out and for everything to be finalized. David couldn't raise any more money to buy them out, and he couldn't find another partner; so in the end he had to sell the boats and close down the business. He went back to his old job as a draughtsman.

A business can be owned in one of four main ways. It may be run by one person as a sole trader; by two or more people in a partnership; as a limited company; or as a co-operative.

1 Sole trader

As the name suggests, one person owns and runs the business. Often this is the way small businesses start off, because there is little or no formality needed for the business structure itself. But obviously the business must comply with the general laws that affect all businesses – for example, planning laws and health and safety legislation. The business may remain small or it may grow and employ any number of other people, but the profits (or losses) belong entirely to the sole owner. Therefore, if your partner is running a business as a sole trader, and you help him or her by giving time or expertise to the business either directly or indirectly, you need to be aware that this does not entitle you to wages unless your partner agrees in advance that you are an employee, or to a share of the profits unless he or she agrees in advance that you are in fact going to be business partners as well as life partners (in which case, see below). On the other hand, you are not liable for your partner's losses as a sole trader unless you have guaranteed any form of credit or loan, or unless you have allowed yourself to appear to other people to be a partner, even though you are not.

You also need to be aware that you will not be entitled to a share of the business if you later split up or your partner dies. This is one of the differences mentioned earlier between marriage and living together. If a couple get divorced, the business may be treated as a family asset and taken into account in the divorce settlement. This is not the case if you are living together.

If either you or your partner are sole traders, you may want to give some thought as to the best way to continue; and if you decide you are both to be involved in the business, you should make sure that your agreement is recorded in writing. It will then be clear whether you are an employee or a business partner.

2 Partnership

You may decide to run the business as partners. Indeed, you may already be business partners before you start living together.

A partnership is a business that has two or more owners. All the partners are entitled to share in the profits and all the partners are jointly and severally responsible for the firm's liabilities. This means that any creditor can sue one or more of the partners for the full amount. It doesn't need any formality to start a partnership. If there is no formal agreement, the provisions of the Partnership Act 1890 will apply. But because it is such an important financial commitment, it is advisable to have a formal partnership deed. Your solicitor will be able to advise you on this. Any business partnership agreement will be separate from any other agreement regulating your personal finances. If you later split up or one of you dies, what happens to the business and your share of it will depend on what it says in your partnership deed. If there is no deed, the available evidence of the terms of the partnership would have to be looked at and the provisions of the Partnership Act applied. It is also possible that you may end your personal relationship, but continue as successful business partners.

3 Limited company

A limited company is very different from the first two types of ownership. This is because it has a separate legal identity from the people involved with it. The company is owned by people who hold shares in it ('the shareholders'). The shareholders appoint directors to run the business, and of course the business may also employ people to work in it in the normal way. The shareholders, directors and employees may change, people leave and new ones take their place, but the company itself continues.

Of course, with a very small business it is likely that the shareholders, directors and employees are the same people.

A limited company need have no more than two persons involved. It must have a minimum of two shareholders and a company secretary and a director. The same two people may fulfil all these functions, and also be the employees doing the day-to-day work of the business.

The main advantage of the company being a separate legal entity is that it is responsible for its own debts. The liability of the shareholders is 'limited' to the amount they have actually put into the company: they are not personally liable for the debts in the same way as a sole trader or partners are. However, for a small company this advantage is likely to be of little practical effect, since banks and anyone providing credit for the company is almost certainly going to ask for a personal guarantee from the directors – at least until the company has established a reputation or can show it has sufficient assets in its own name to cover borrowing and debts. Until then, the directors are likely to have to guarantee loans and credit and are therefore in a very similar position to a sole trader or partner. The decision as to whether you should set up a limited company to run your business is one for which you should seek advice from your accountant and solicitor. You should be careful to make sure, however, that if you are asked – for example, by a bank – to provide a personal guarantee, you fully understand the implications, particularly if it involves putting up your home as security. Bear in mind that if your home is to be used as security, both joint owners will have to agree and will have to sign the necessary documents.

If you separate or if one of you dies, the company will continue in existence. If you are the only shareholders, one of you could try to buy the other out, but the other is not obliged to sell. If you are both directors, as directors are appointed and dismissed by the shareholders, what happens to you will depend on your respective shareholdings and therefore your voting rights. Employees can be dismissed by the directors. If one of you has died, his or her voting rights will be exercised by his or her personal representatives/beneficiaries.

4 Co-operative

A small number of businesses are set up and run as co-operative ventures. There is no single legal definition, but the basis of a co-operative is that it is owned and run by the people who work in it, and usually only people who work in the business are entitled to become part owners. If you and your partner are interested in forming a business co-operative, you are likely to have already given it a lot of thought. In addition, there are a number of organizations that offer help and advice. As the philosophy is that those working in the firm each own a part of it, your entitlement is unlikely to be directly affected by a split up with your partner or the death of one of you, although, as with other forms of ownership, you need to check this at the outset.

FOUR: Does Living Together Affect Your State Benefits?

The short answer is yes, because if your relationship is basically like that of husband and wife, the Department of Social Security (DSS) will treat you as one family unit.

The decision about whether you are living together as 'husband and wife' will be made by an adjudication officer from information gathered by the visiting officer. A number of matters are taken into account, such as whether you live in the same household – that is, live together the whole time, share meals, and do jobs around the home for each other – whether it is an established relationship; whether you share household expenses; whether there is a sexual relationship (you cannot be asked this, but you can volunteer the information if it would help); whether you are caring for a child or children of whom you are the parents; and how other people see the relationship. You can appeal against such a decision within three months.

1 Income Support (formerly Supplementary Benefit)

If you are living together, then, although either of you can claim, the claim must be for both of you and *neither* of you should be doing more than twenty-four hours per week of paid work. You will be treated as one unit so far as housing costs and any children of either or both of you living with you are concerned.

2 Family Credit (formerly Family Income Supplement (FIS))

This is a social security benefit paid to you if you are working twenty-four hours per week or more on a low income with at least one child aged under 16.

If you are living together, you can still claim as long as your *joint* earnings remain at a low income level.

3 Housing Benefit

This is a benefit paid to you if you are on a low income to help you with your rent and community charge. If you are living together, you will be treated as one family unit.

4 Child Benefit and One Parent Benefit

Child Benefit is one benefit that is not affected by living together.

One Parent Benefit is paid to you if you are solely responsible for one or more children living with you, and will not be paid if you are living together.

5 Widow's Pension

Your right to a DSS Widow's Pension, or Widowed Mother's Allowance from your previous marriage, may be suspended if you live with someone (unless you are already over 65 or over 60 and retired).

On the other hand, you will have no entitlement to a Widow's Pension as a result of your partner dying because, of course, you were not married to each other.

FIVE: Previous Relationships

Does living together affect you if you or your partner are separated, divorced or divorcing previous partners?

If you are separated, but still own the matrimonial home jointly with your spouse, you should consider asking your solicitor about severing the joint ownership. If the matrimonial home is in your spouse's sole name, you should discuss with your solicitor the protection of your rights in the property.

On divorce, orders are usually made dealing with maintenance, lump sums and property.

1 Does living together affect the maintenance you receive?

If you are receiving maintenance for yourself under a court order, then it is quite likely that the court order will provide for those payments to stop if you live with someone or do so for a particular period of time. You should check the wording of the order.

If the order does not make such a provision, it is still open to the person who pays to apply to the court for the cancellation of the order on the basis that you are receiving financial support from your present partner. If the application is made, the court would make enquiries as to the extent, if any, of that support.

If you are receiving maintenance for a child or children under a court order, then living together will not affect the payment. If the person who pays subsequently makes an application to the court for reduction of the amount, then any support you receive from your partner would be taken into account.

2 Does living together affect the maintenance you pay?

You may be paying maintenance under a court order for a spouse, ex-spouse or children of a marriage or previous relationship. Your partner's income and contribution to household expenses will be taken into account when assessing what money you have available, although your incomes will not actually be added together for the purposes of any calculations. If, on the other hand, you are supporting your partner financially, such support will also be taken into account when assessing how much maintenance you should pay.

3 Does living together affect lump sum and property orders?

If you start living together soon after a lump sum or property order has been made in your favour, and you knew or were reasonably certain when the order was made that you intended to do this and failed to disclose the intention to your divorcing spouse, then s/he can apply to the court for the order to be varied or revoked.

If you are continuing to live in a home you own jointly with your ex-spouse, it will sometimes be a condition that the property is sold and the proceeds divided (or that you make a payment to your ex-spouse in respect of his/her share in the property) if you live with someone. Again, you should check the wording of the order.

SIX: You and Your Children

1 Parenting

The care and upbringing of children of your relationship will, on a practical level, be a matter for agreement between you. Strictly, only the mother has legal rights in respect of those children including, for example, the right to sign a form of consent to an operation, to decide what religion they should be brought up in, or what school they should go to; but, in practice, this distinction is not always observed.

You can agree between you, while you are living together, that the father should share the rights and duties with the mother. Such an agreement would only be enforced by the court if the court felt it would be beneficial to the child. There seems to be no reason why you should not make an enforceable agreement while you are living together, even in respect of any future child of yours, in a living together agreement.

2 Shared parenting

Under the Children Act 1989, only parts of which are in force at the time of writing, a father will be able to apply to the court for an order that he have parental responsibility for the child and, if granted, would share parental responsibility with the mother.

Alternatively, under the Act you could both enter into a 'parental responsibility agreement'. In order to ensure that you both understand the importance and effect of this agreement and to ensure that the mother has not been put under undue pressure to enter the agreement, it is proposed that a 'parental responsibility agreement' must be made formally in a prescribed form. Any such order or agreement may be ended by the court on the application of the person having parental responsibility, or the child – if the court is satisfied that he or she has sufficient understanding to make the application.

Parental responsibility is defined as 'all the rights, duties, powers, responsibilities and authority which by law a parent of a child has in relation to the child and his or her property'. This is subject to the decision in the Gillick case in 1986 that older children have a right to decide matters for themselves provided they are sufficiently mature to understand fully the implications. As Lord Denning said, a parent's right (of custody) is a dwindling right. 'It starts with a right of control and ends with little more than advice.'

3 Registration of birth

The birth of a child must by law be registered within forty-two days at the register office for the district where the baby was born.

Will both the mother's and father's details be included in the register?

If you are the parents of a baby and you are not married to each other, then the mother's details – that is, name, address and occupation – will always be entered.

The father's details can also be entered at the time or subsequently, but only in the following circumstances:

(a) At the joint request of the mother and father, and if you both go along to the register office, you can both be entered.
(b) At the request of one, provided he or she has a declaration in a prescribed form made by him or her as to who is the father of the child, and a statutory declaration by the other confirming who is the father.
(c) At the request of one on production of a certified copy of a court order giving the man parental rights or requiring him to make financial provision. (If the child is over 16, then you do need the child's written consent to the registration.)

Can the registration be altered later?

If the child has already been registered but no person has been registered as the father, the registrar can re-register the birth so as to show a particular person as the father if (a) or (b) above is satisfied.

4 Surnames

As a general rule, you can use any surname you like, unless you do so with the intention to defraud. This means that if you decide to live with your partner and want to adopt his or her name, you can do so, subject to the point made above. Indeed, you can both adopt an entirely different name if you prefer. For instance, you could invent a new name based on a combination of your names as one Danish couple living together did, according to a newspaper report.

However, there is no obligation to adopt someone else's name, even if you are married. Many women nowadays retain their maiden names after marriage, particularly if they have a career which they started before they were married.

In the same way, you can give your children any name you wish. This might be your own, your partner's or a combination of the two. But there are differences between the rights of parents who are not married to one another and parents who are, or were, married to one another.

A mother who is not married (and never has been married) to the father of her children has all the rights in relation to those children. There are some steps the father can take to obtain rights, but these are dealt with later. The rights the mother has include the right to choose the child's name – and change it later if she wishes, usually by statutory declaration or deed poll. There is nothing the father can do about this as the mother does not need his consent. Obviously, a child who is over 18 can choose the name he or she wishes to be known by but, until then, the mother can choose.

If the parents were married to one another either at the time of or after the birth of their child, both will have equal rights in relation to the child. This will include the right to choose the child's name. It is usually only after divorce that this can give rise to problems when the parent with whom the child is living is the mother and she remarries or forms a new relationship and has further children, who have her new partner's name. Either she or the children of the previous marriage may then wish to change the children's surname.

However, the standard form of custody order in most divorce courts states that the children's names cannot be changed without the other parent's consent or the consent of the court while they are under 18, except in the case of a girl if she marries under that age.

If you do wish to change your name, you can do so by making a statutory declaration or deed poll. Your solicitor can prepare either of these documents for you.

SEVEN: Does Living Together Affect How You Are Taxed?

1 Income Tax

You will, of course, continue to be taxed as two separate people; you will each continue to have a 'personal allowance' to set against your income. After changes in April 1990 that provided for married couples to be taxed separately, there is now little difference from an income tax point of view between married and unmarried couples.

Since 1 August 1988 tax relief on mortgage interest payments is limited to a £30,000 loan limit per property. If the property and mortgage are joint, the limit and the related tax relief will be apportioned between the joint owners. Unlike married couples, partners are not able to transfer the mortgage relief – for example, if one partner stops work.

2 Capital Gains Tax

This is a tax payable on the gain you make on an asset when you dispose of it. 'Disposal' can include selling it or transferring it by gift. There are no special exemptions for partners, as there are for husbands and wives. Therefore, any transfer of an asset to your partner may result in a liability to Capital Gains Tax. The annual exemption (at present

£5,000) may help, but putting payment off until sale – 'hold over' relief – is in general no longer available.

Main residence exemption

Your home is exempt from Capital Gains Tax provided it is your main residence, so that transfer of part or the whole of it is not taxable. If one of you leaves a home to move in with the other, perhaps letting your own property to someone else, then you need to be aware that this may no longer count as your main residence. It will depend on the circumstances.

3 Inheritance Tax

This is payable on the value of all transfers made on death (or within seven years of death) that exceed the 'tax free' limit set by the government, usually in the Budget. When introduced in 1986 the limit was £71,000, by 1990 it had risen to £128,000. Certain lifetime transfers may result in liability.

Again, it is less easy for partners to make tax savings by lifetime transfers to each other. These would be exempt if between husband and wife. However, planning ahead, and use of the available exemptions, may be used to minimize the tax bill on death.

Note: The above points are simple outlines of complex tax legislation, and expert advice should always be sought before any transaction is undertaken.

SECTION THREE:
What Happens if You Separate?

Introduction

A separation may come about in any one of a number of ways. You may both agree that you are not getting on, that there is no future in your relationship, and that you ought to part. Alternatively, only one of you may wish to end the arrangement, in which case that person may tell the other or may simply leave. However it happens, it is going to mean splitting up your finances as well as separating physically. Even if you have kept your money and belongings separate throughout the relationship, it is going to be the case that you are both living under only one roof. However amicable your separation may be, it is unlikely that you will both want to continue living there. If you own the property, one or both of you will want to raise some cash from it with which to start again.

Remember that if you own the home as joint owners and are splitting up, you may wish to talk to your solicitor about severing the joint ownership (to protect your share if you die suddenly) and make a will, or even make a new one (see Section 4).

ONE: Your Home

So what is to happen to the home?

Much will depend on whether you own the home (alone or together) or whether it is rented.

1 If you own your home

Are you going to have to sell? This will depend mainly on (i) how you own the house, and (ii) whether or not you have come to any written agreement with your partner about what is to happen when you separate. This may have been recorded in a document such as a declaration of trust or living together agreement.

(a) If the house is in joint names

It is more than likely that you will have to sell so that you can each have your share of the proceeds. It is possible for one of you to buy the other out, finances permitting, but if the other refuses to be bought out the property may have to be sold. If you want out and your partner does not, you could apply to the court for an order that the property be sold. The court usually takes the view that the purpose for which you bought the property together has come to an end, and so the house should be sold and the proceeds distributed.

An application to court is almost always going to take a considerable length of time and can cost a lot of money. It would involve setting out in written form your claim for an order for sale and the reasons for it, and the documents would be submitted to the court with a court fee. Your former partner may then set out in writing his or her side of the case; then both of you will have to disclose all the documentary evidence on which you intend to rely, and valuations and mortgage redemption figures may have to be obtained. If no other information is required, there would then be a court hearing that you would have to attend and then a decision would be made. If you lose, the court could order you to pay your partner's legal expenses. You may qualify for legal aid to help you to take your case to court, but you may have to pay back your legal expenses to the Legal Aid Fund out of any money received at the end of the case, or when the property is sold. If you win, your partner may be ordered to pay your legal expenses, but there may be practical difficulties getting the money.

One way of avoiding all these problems is to set out in a living together agreement what you would want to happen to the home. For example, that the one who wishes to remain should have, say, four months to complete the purchase of the other's share or, if both of you want to stay, that the first of you able to raise the finance should be able to buy the other out. This may sound brutal, but if you both agree to it from the outset at least you know where you stand.

If you have children, the question of a home may be more

critical. It is of course possible to provide in the living-together agreement that the partner caring for the children should have first option to purchase the other's share. If you cannot agree what should happen, you could apply to the court and the court may decide that the main reason for buying the house was to provide a home for the family – thus the partner caring for the children should be allowed to stay for a specified period. It is not automatically the case that you will be allowed to stay until the youngest child is 17 or finishes full-time education.

(b) If the home is in one name, but you both have a share

If you have made a deed of trust declaring that you both have an interest in the property even though only one name is actually on the title deeds, then you can provide in a living together agreement that, for example, if yours is the name on the deeds you should have first option to buy your partner's share. If you are not able to complete the purchase within, say, four months, then your partner can buy your share. If neither can go ahead, then the house would be sold.

(c) If you have no share in the home

If the home is in your partner's name, then the law says that you live there at his or her invitation or 'licence'. In other words, you can only live there as long as your partner agrees. If your relationship breaks down it is more than likely that your partner will simply terminate the licence and will require you to leave. If you refuse, then your partner can make an application to the court which may result in you being evicted.

To avoid this, you and your partner can provide in a living together agreement that you should be allowed, say, three months to find somewhere else to live.

You will see from the above how important it is that you think about what would happen if you separated. You may have given up a home to move in with your partner and you could then find yourself having to leave. Suppose you leave your parents to buy a property jointly with your partner, and with joint resources you are able to take on a reasonably sized mortgage and buy a lovely home to have a secure roof over your heads. Then things go wrong and you find that you are left with, perhaps, a small lump sum. As a single person, the size of the mortgage you can take out is much less, and perhaps you cannot afford to purchase another property on your own. You are faced with renting or going home to parents. (See Example B.)

Example B

Pauline couldn't wait to leave home. She didn't get on well with her stepfather and she had to share a room with her sister. She had known David since school, and they had been going out together for five years. They had saved up a deposit and, as David worked in the bank, they had been able to buy a new house with reasonably low mortgage repayments. Pauline spent many happy hours choosing the colour schemes and furnishings. After a couple of years it was clear that they couldn't live together. Pauline's pride and joy had to be sold and, on her own, she couldn't afford to buy anything else. She couldn't face going home, so she rented a bedsitter at an extortionate rent.

Suppose you have sold your previous home to move in with your partner. You may have invested the proceeds of sale in a building society account, for example; but if things go wrong you may find that your investment has not kept pace with increasing property prices and is not sufficient to enable you to buy again. (See Example C.)

Example C

Susan had a disastrous marriage and was subsequently divorced. The house was sold and she received £10,000. She could get a mortgage of £30,000 and planned to buy herself a flat for £40,000. Then she met Oliver. Having just got over the divorce, she wanted to be cautious. She put the £10,000 in a building society. Things didn't work out, and she left Oliver two years later. That flat she wanted now cost £80,000.

These are realities you would have to face, and sometimes there is nothing you can do to avoid them; but at least if you are aware of them, you will go into the arrangement with your eyes open. With a little forethought and advance planning, you might be able to reach an agreement so that you both have a good chance of salvaging something from the relationship.

Obviously if you have children, the question of accommodation is critical; and if you give up a home to move in with your partner, bringing with you children of a previous relationship, it is vital that you consider the security of your accommodation.

2 How much will you get out of the home?

If you cannot continue living under the same roof, then it will be important to you to know as quickly as possible how much you are going to get out of the home so as to be able to start afresh somewhere else. This will really depend on how you own your home.

(a) If you are joint owners

If you are joint owners as described in Chapter 1 of Section 2, then you will be entitled to half each of the net proceeds of sale. The net proceeds of sale means the amount remaining of the sale price after payment of the amount outstanding on the mortgage, the estate agent's charges, and the solicitor's conveyancing costs. You will receive half each, even if one of you put in a lot more than the other. This may have been at the beginning by paying all or part of the deposit, or because you bought the home below market price because of a local authority tenant's discount or because a member of your family sold it to you at an undervalue. (See Example D.) Alternatively, this may have been during the relationship by paying more of the mortgage or paying for improvements.

Example D

Kevin's grandmother left her house to Kevin's father when she died. It was worth about £60,000 at the time. Kevin's father didn't need it and was going to put it up for sale, but Kevin and his girlfriend, Julie, were looking for somewhere to live. They couldn't raise £60,000, but they could go to £40,000 with a 100 per cent mortgage. Kevin's father agreed to let them have it for that and it was transferred into their joint names as 'joint owners'. Julie was unemployed and Kevin paid the mortgage and all the bills. Eighteen months later, Julie went home to Mum and insisted the house be sold and the profit divided equally between them. It sold for £70,000, so Julie came out with almost £15,000. Kevin and his father were not very pleased.

(b) If you are owners in common

If you are owners in common as described in Chapter 1 of Section 2, then your entitlement will depend on whether the title deeds say in what shares you own the property. If the title deeds do state the shares, then it is more than likely that that will determine your entitlement – whether or not your actual contributions to the property differ from those declared shares. Thus, if the title deeds declare that you own the property as owners in common in equal shares, then you will be entitled to half each of the net proceeds of sale.

If the title deeds do not describe in what shares you own the property, then you may be entitled to half each, but the whole matter is open for argument. Unless you and your partner can agree, the matter will have to be decided by the court. Bear in mind that the emotional upheaval that normally accompanies a separation is not conducive to rational and logical discussion and agreement. In the heat of the moment you or your partner may forget what you originally agreed or your recollections of the agreement may not exactly coincide. With the passage of time, and even with the best will in the world, you may not be able to remember accurately what it was you agreed. This is how disputes end up in court.

The court will try to determine what your intentions were at the time you bought the property or when you invested any large sums of money in it, and will also look at what actual contributions you each made.

To enable the court to make a decision, you will have to set out in writing what you believe the agreement between you was, what contributions you say you have made, and what share you are claiming. Your partner will of course do the same. You will both have to produce any evidence you have to support what you say. Unless you have kept meticulous records of everything you have paid over the years, you could be in difficulty. There will then be a court hearing that you will both have to attend, together with any witnesses, such as family to give evidence of a loan or contributions, or an expert to give evidence as to the value of the property. Clearly this can take a considerable time and cost a lot of money. Quite apart from solicitors' and barristers' fees, there will be court fees; and you may have to pay a valuer to attend a hearing.

It is likely that with the trauma of separation you will each have very different interpretations of what your intentions were, and the court will have to decide who to believe. You can imagine that this is a very risky business. In the absence of detailed accounts and agreed evidence of intentions, the court will have to take a broad view and divide the net proceeds of sale between you on the basis of its best guess as to your contributions and intentions.

You may not feel that to enter into lengthy and costly court proceedings with the likelihood that a rough division will be made at the end of the day is very sensible. We agree. That is why we feel it is important that you should determine your shares in the property by recording your intentions in a living together agreement and a deed of trust, as described in Chapter 1 of Section 2, while you are still happy together. If you have done this, you will both have a very good idea of the amount each of you will receive. If your circumstances change, you can always have a new agreement and deed of trust.

(c) If the home is in one name

If your partner has the home in his or her sole name, then he or she may well keep the entire proceeds of sale. Suppose you have sold your own property to move in with your partner, and you have used some or all of your money for some new kitchen units, or perhaps for central heating or double glazing. Unless you have recorded an agreement that your contribution entitles you to a share in the property, you might just as well have poured your money down the drain;

because even if you do manage to recover your investment, it could be a costly exercise. On separation, if you couldn't agree that you were entitled to a share, you would have to apply to court to prove that your contribution had added to the value of the property or reduced the amount outstanding on the mortgage, *and* that when you made the payment your joint intention was that you would thereby acquire a share. Imagine how difficult that could be without anything in writing and no independent witnesses. (See Example E.)

Example E

When Patsie moved into Mark's house, the kitchen was an original 1930s one. Mark infrequently ate at home, so it hadn't bothered him. Patsie offered to spend her redundancy money on some new kitchen units and appliances. Mark said she could if she wanted to. The arguments started almost as soon as the work was done, and within three months Patsie had left. Mark refused to pay her anything and Patsie couldn't afford to take him to court.

A year later she saw the house advertised for sale as 'including luxury kitchen'.

So remember, if you move in with someone who owns his or her own property or agree when it is bought that it should be in your partner's sole name, then you should discuss what share, if any, you are to have; and, if you make a contribution, whether this is to affect the size of your share. Once agreed, you should make sure that it is properly recorded. (See Example F.) If you have no written record, then you are likely to face a lengthy and costly court case (see (b) above) and still end up with a result that probably won't please either of you.

Example F

When Ann met Peter she thought all her dreams had come true – a terrific relationship, a penthouse flat, cottage in the country, and lifestyle to go with it. She gave up a promising career as an interior designer and threw herself into helping Peter build up his business, entertaining clients, and looking after the homes. She never thought about securing an interest in his property. Twelve years later, Peter met a model and Ann was homeless.

Nowhere to live, no income, and no right to a share in Peter's homes or business. Having made no financial contribution to the properties, it wasn't even worth Ann taking him to court.

It is possible that you might move in with someone who owns his or her own property, and you might agree that you will never have a share even if you do make a contribution. If you do this, you must understand that you may end up with nothing, and you should only go ahead after very serious consideration and possibly independent legal advice. If you have sold your own property to move in with someone and invested the money, then remember that it is unlikely that your investment will have kept pace with increasing property prices.

3 If the home is rented

(a) If the home is rented in your sole name

In this instance, your partner has no right to occupy, and if he/she refuses to leave you could apply to the court for an order that he/she must go.

(b) If the home is rented in your partner's sole name

Here, *you* have no right to stay. If your partner has left the property, you may, in certain circumstances, have the right to have the tenancy transferred to you, if your partner has agreed to this.

(c) If the home is rented in joint names

In this case, you are both entitled to occupy. If one leaves, the other is entitled to remain. In that case, the tenancy should be transferred into the name of the one who stays, as otherwise you will both remain liable for the rent. You can set out in a living together agreement what you want to happen. For example, if the home is in joint names and you cannot agree who should stay, that preference should be given to the partner caring for a child, or the decision made that you both should leave.

4 It is never too late

If you have been living together for some time when you read this, and realize that you are in a vulnerable position, it is not too late to do something about it. So long as you are able to agree, you can record in writing how you want your previous and future contributions reflected in your shares in the property.

TWO: Contents and Money

1 Contents

If you separate, you are going to have to decide who has what of the contents of your home. This can often cause more arguments than anything else.

The basic principles are:

(a) Anything you owned before you started living together and brought with you to the relationship remains yours.
(b) Anything you buy with your own money remains yours.
(c) Anything given to you personally remains yours.
(d) Anything bought out of joint money belongs to you both.

Now those principles in themselves may not always be satisfactory. It could be that the financial arrangements you have with your partner are such that one of you buys all the contents while the other pays the household bills. You may not think it fair that the one who has paid all the household bills should not be entitled to any contents. You can set out in a living together agreement that you want all items purchased during the relationship to be considered joint property, whoever paid for them.

Then again there may be specific items that one of you

would want to retain whatever happens. For example, perhaps you are particularly interested in photography or hi-fi and have bought a lot of expensive equipment. In that case, you could think about stating in a living together agreement that although, in general, all contents should belong to you jointly, your photography equipment and hi-fi system should belong to you alone. In addition, you might decide that although in general all contents should belong to you jointly, any items costing more than a certain amount should belong to the person who bought them.

If you agree that some or all of the contents should be considered jointly owned, then what happens when you separate? There is no easy answer. If you cannot agree who has what, then they may all have to be sold and the proceeds divided between you. Second-hand items do not generally fetch a high price, and that in itself might be sufficient incentive to ensure that you do agree between you who is to have what.

2 What about items purchased on credit?

With the increasing use of credit in recent years, many readers will no doubt have purchased items for the home on credit. The most important thing to remember is that if you purchase items on credit you will remain liable to repay that credit, whether or not you still have the item.

Suppose on separation your partner is going to have the care of the children. He or she will probably want to keep the washing machine, but what if you bought it on credit and only your name is on the credit agreement? He or she will have the washing machine, but you will still have to make the repayments. You may not see why you should continue to pay for something without having the use or benefit of it. This is perhaps understandable, but the credit company can legally oblige you to repay the debt even though you no longer have the washing machine. It is important to remember when purchasing anything on credit that credit agreements cannot generally be transferred from one person to another.

If the credit is in joint names, you both remain liable for the repayments and the items belong to you both. The credit company can legally oblige either of you to repay the whole debt and not just half, but in practice they will probably enforce judgement only against the one who seems most likely to be able to pay. If you have been called upon to pay the whole amount yourself, you could claim a contribution from your partner if his or her name was on the agreement, but if the credit company did not feel optimistic about getting the money out of him or her, are your chances really much better, looked at realistically?

Remember, if you have guaranteed a credit purchase in your partner's name and your partner defaults, the lender will look to you for the money so that, for example, if it was a motorbike, you may find that you are forced to pay a substantial sum of money for something you have never had and are never likely to see again. If your partner and the motorbike are still around, you can claim the money back from her. But if she couldn't afford to pay the finance company, is it any more likely that she will be able to pay you? The only bright spot on that particular horizon would be that you could claim the motorbike if you have paid for it.

If you have bought items using a joint bank loan, overdraft facility or a joint credit card, then you both remain liable for the repayments – regardless of who has the items. You will have to try and agree who is going to have what, and this is not always easy.

One way to avoid disputes would be to agree in advance who should have what or, if that is not possible, agree that the items are jointly owned. Then, if you cannot agree who should have what, they should all be sold and the proceeds divided.

3 What about credit cards?

Apart from specific items bought with a credit card, there is the question of responsibility for repayments on such cards. Obviously, so far as the credit company is concerned, the account holder will be responsible whatever happens. This means that:

(a) If you have a card in your sole name, you will be responsible to the company.
(b) If you have a card in joint names, you will both be responsible to the company.
(c) If you have a card with your partner as authorized user, you, and not your partner, will be responsible to the company.

However, it may be that purchases were made on one or other card without too much thought as to who was legally responsible for the repayments, and then on separation there can be argument.

Suppose you pay for a joint holiday on your own credit card a month before you separate. You may not be too happy about having to pay it all back yourself without a contribution from your partner. You can agree between yourselves in a living together agreement how you are going to make any credit card repayments. You may agree that the use of a credit card is an integral part of your financial arrangements, and that apportionment of the repayments should be made accordingly.

4 What about family loans?

If you have not agreed responsibility for repayment of family loans, this can often cause problems on separation. Suppose your parents lent you both some money to pay off some debts and then you separate, your partner will probably not feel inclined to pay anything to your parents and will probably claim that the money was a gift or a loan to you personally. Your parents will claim that the whole loan should be repaid, or that at least your partner should pay his or her half. (See Example G.) Parents or other relatives making such a loan should really enter into a written agreement with both of you recording the loan and providing for repayment. Even if they do not, it is sensible to agree between yourselves at the outset how any such loans should be repaid.

Example G

Cynthia and Brian had lived together for five years, and Cynthia had just given up work for the birth of their first child when Brian was made redundant. Six months on and still no sign of a job, they were getting into serious debt. Brian didn't want Cynthia to worry about it, and took out a loan from a finance company with a very high rate of interest. Things went from bad to worse and eventually he had to tell Cynthia. Her parents offered to lend them the money to clear off the loan and all their other debts, and they gratefully accepted. However, the fact that Brian had not told Cynthia what was happening annoyed her, and from then on their relationship deteriorated. They split up and Cynthia's parents wanted Brian to repay half the loan. He claimed it was a gift to Cynthia. There was nothing in writing. Cynthia and her parents faced a costly court battle to get any money back.

---

5 Bank and building society accounts and other capital assets

On separation, any such accounts or assets in your sole name remain yours and any in your partner's sole name belong to your partner. This is the general rule, but the position may be different if you have paid any money towards the asset or into the account. Most problems arise with joint accounts or jointly owned investments or other joint capital assets. Accounts in joint names are not necessarily held in equal shares unless you have made it clear that that is what you both intend. Banks will often freeze a joint account as soon as they know of any problem in the relationship, and may refuse to release any money until both of you agree on how it is to be divided. On separation, you may feel that you are entitled to more than half, and that could mean having to go to court to sort it out.

If you set out in a letter to the bank or a living together agreement in what proportions you own the account, then that should settle the matter.

6 Businesses

If, when you split up, you are jointly running a business, then what you will each be entitled to, as with other property, will be decided on the basis of what you put into the business in money and what your joint intentions were. This is quite different from the position if you are divorcing, when the court may order that one spouse receives a share of the value of the business even if he or she has not contributed directly to it. You will have to prove any actual contributions. (See Example H.)

Example H

When Penny met Dave he had recently started his own business as a plumber, but was struggling to do the paperwork and was losing a lot of business through never being at home to answer the phone. Penny sold her flat and moved in with him. She worked day and night helping Dave to build up the business until they had twenty people working for them and a shop selling plumbing and heating parts and materials. Penny always regarded it as their business, and she was proud that all her hard work had resulted in this success.

However, she was horrified to discover that Dave had run up gambling debts. Their relationship was never the same and quite soon Penny realized they would have to separate. She thought that she probably had no rights to stay in Dave's house, but was staggered to learn that she had no right to claim any part of the value of the business, despite all her hard work, because she hadn't put any money into it.

---

7 What about pets?

Basically, if you paid for the pets you can keep them. If you both paid for them, then you will have to try and agree between you who is to have them; if you cannot agree, they will have to be sold and the proceeds divided between you.

THREE: Maintenance

1 Are you entitled to maintenance?

On separation, you are not entitled to any maintenance from your partner, even if he or she has supported you for years. You may have given up work at his or her insistence and perhaps lost valuable years in your career, but you will not be entitled to any maintenance. You may be unable to work and support yourself through ill health or because you are caring for a young child, but you will still not be entitled to any maintenance. The notion of 'palimony' has not yet reached this side of the Atlantic.

Furthermore, you will not be entitled to maintenance for any children who are not children of the relationship. Suppose you have a baby from a previous relationship, but then you start living with your partner and you live as a family for the next ten years. Your partner treats that child as his own and supports him or her as part of the family. On separation, you would still not be entitled to any maintenance for that child.

With regard to children of your relationship with your partner, see Chapter 5 on p. 108.

2 Will you have to pay maintenance?

If there are no children of the relationship, you will not have to pay maintenance to your former partner. But where there are children and they are living with your former partner and he or she is on Income Support, the DSS will seek payment from you, not only for the children but also for your partner as carer. This will not apply if your former partner comes off income support.

3 What about social security?

You will revert to being regarded as a single person for assessment of your entitlement to social security benefits. You should notify the DSS as quickly as possible so that a reassessment can be made. If you qualified for Family Credit while living together, then this will continue for the remainder of the period for which it is payable.

FOUR: Violence

1 What can you do if your partner is violent?

The first thing to do is to call the police. They should normally answer an emergency call for help and that in itself should help to defuse the situation.

One problem is that the police are generally reluctant to interfere with what they call 'domestics'. The reasons for this are partly historical. Because a woman was the property of her husband (like his animals), she could be treated accordingly. Because an 'Englishman's home is his castle', the police have limited rights of entry. There are also practical reasons, in that police become weary of the number of prosecutions that fail because the victim does not pursue the case or becomes reconciled with the offender.

There are signs of improvement in the attitudes of the police, although it is still the case that in some areas domestic violence is taken more seriously than in others.

Your partner will only be arrested or charged if he or she has committed a crime, but there are problems with criminal proceedings. In less serious cases of common assault, the victim can press the charge. In more serious cases, the police will bring the charge, but the victim will be the main, and sometimes the only, witness. Victims may decide not to pursue the case for a number of reasons. They may not want to be the cause of the offender going to prison, particularly because of the effect this may have on any children of the partnership. Alternatively, a prison sentence may, in the particular circumstances, be unlikely, leaving the offender a potential threat and the victim feeling more vulnerable; therefore, pressing charges may seem pointless. However, such charges do have the immediate effect of the offender being either kept in custody or subject to bail conditions. These may include not going near the victim until the trial, and this can sometimes remove the immediate threat to the victim's safety.

2 Civil injunctions

If the victim decides for whatever reason that criminal proceedings are not the appropriate course of action or that he or she wishes to obtain an order from the civil court as well, then it may be possible to apply to the county court for an injunction. This is a court order *prohibiting* the violent partner from doing something, or *requiring* him or her to do something.

3 Injunctions under the Domestic Violence and Matrimonial Proceedings Act

If you are living together in the same household as 'husband and wife', then you can apply to the county court for an order:

(a) restraining your partner from molesting you and/or a child living with you;
(b) excluding your partner from the home or part of the home;
(c) requiring your partner to permit you to enter and remain in the home or part of it.

You can use this procedure if you were living together as 'husband and wife' at the time of the last incident referred to in your application.

You cannot use this procedure if:

1 You are a homosexual or lesbian couple.
2 You have been living under the same roof for convenience rather than in a husband – wife relationship.
3 You have already separated at the time of the last incident.

In these circumstances, there are alternative procedures available; see below.

What does molesting mean?

To obtain an injunction restraining your partner from molesting you, there must be real evidence of molestation. What conduct amounts to molestation will depend on the circumstances and the court will have to decide in each individual case. Violence is a form of molestation. However, there can be molestation without violence or threat of it, provided the behaviour affects your physical and/or mental health or that of any children living with you. It has been said to include any conduct that can properly be regarded as such a degree of harassment as to call for the intervention of the court.

Can you get your partner out?

To obtain an order obliging your partner to move out of the home (known as an exclusion order or ouster injunction), you have to convince the court that, in all the circumstances, such an order is right. The court will take into account various factors including behaviour, the needs of any children, and your needs and financial resources and those of your partner. Orders requiring your partner to allow you to move back in are usually made with orders excluding your partner from the home.

How quickly can you get an injunction?

In cases of real emergency, the court will make an order restraining your partner from molesting you (but not ordering him or her to move out) before he or she has been informed of your application, and thus without hearing his or her side of the story. However, this will only happen where there is a real immediate danger of serious injury or irreparable damage. Such an order will only be effective from the time your partner receives it, and will be valid for a limited period of time. There will be another court hearing at which your partner will have the opportunity of putting his or her case. The court will then decide whether or not to continue the order.

How long does this protection last?

Orders of the above type are normally only made to last for a limited period – for example, three months initially. It is open to either party to apply to the court at any time during the period for an extension or a discharge (cancellation) of the order.

What happens if your partner disobeys the order?

If such an order is made against your partner and he or she disobeys it, then it is possible to apply to the court for an order committing your partner to prison. In very exceptional circumstances, the court will make an order without your partner being informed of your application and without hearing his or her side of the story. This is extremely rare and will only normally be when your partner has blatantly ignored the court order and continues to ignore it or threatens to do so. Committal to prison is very much a last resort, and the court will normally try to give your partner every opportunity to mend his or her ways before imposing a prison sentence.

Powers of arrest

If your partner has caused 'actual bodily harm' to you or a child living with you, and is likely to do so again, then the court may attach a power of arrest to the injunction. Again, this is exceptional and will only be added in the most serious of cases. It enables a police officer to arrest without warrant a person whom he has reasonable cause for suspecting of being in breach of the injunction. The arrested person must be brought before a judge within twenty-four hours, and must not be released within that time unless the judge permits it. You would then explain to the judge what your partner had done in breach of the injunction, and the judge might then fine your partner or commit him or her to prison for contempt of court.

4 Alternative procedures

If you are not able to obtain an injunction under the Domestic Violence and Matrimonial Proceedings Act because you have never, or not for some time, lived together as 'husband and wife', or because you are a homosexual or lesbian couple, then the only way you can obtain an injunction is to bring an action against your partner for damages (i.e. compensation) for assault, trespass or nuisance. This is simply the procedure by which you can bring an application for an injunction before the court, and does not mean that you have to pursue the claim for damages to its end. The same sort of orders can be made as above, and again they can be made in exceptional and urgent cases without your partner first being informed. Your partner can be committed to prison for breach of the order.

5 How much will it cost?

This will depend on whether you qualify for legal aid and, if not, how much your solicitor charges. You should ask your solicitor. If you qualify for legal aid, emergency legal aid is available for really urgent cases.

6 Compensation for criminal injuries

The Criminal Injuries Compensation Board will pay compensation to any person who sustains personal injury as a direct result of a crime of violence where compensation of not less than £750 would be awarded. In most 'domestic' situations, a claim can only be made if the following apply:

(a) the victim and offender were living together as 'husband and wife' at the time of the injury, and
(b) the offender has been prosecuted or there are good reasons why not, and
(c) the injury was one for which compensation of not less than £750 would be awarded, and
(d) the parties stopped living together in the same household before applying for compensation and seem unlikely to live together again.

Living together agreement

There is nothing you can say in a living together agreement which can prevent you from seeking the protection of the court.

FIVE: Children

1 What about children of the relationship?

On separation, the future care and support of any children of your relationship are going to be your major concern. You will have to try and agree what are going to be the best arrangements that can be made for the children. The welfare of the children is the first and paramount consideration, because this is how the court will view it.

2 What does the law say about custody and access?

If you are a father, who is not married to the mother of your child, you have no automatic rights to custody or access. (See Example I.)

Example I

Phil and Sandy had a lovely baby called Jessica. Phil was a freelance illustrator working from home and, as Sandy was on the career ladder in a large firm of accountants, Phil offered to look after Jessica while Sandy went back to work. Phil was the proudest father in the world and did everything for her. Four years later Phil and Sandy separated after a very nasty row, and Sandy went to stay with a friend. Then Sandy found herself a flat, employed a nanny, and went to collect Jessica from Phil. He was devastated and refused to let her go. He called the police. He also telephoned a friend who was a solicitor. Both told him the same thing. He had no right to keep Jessica. If he wanted to have custody of her, he would have to fight it out in court.

If you cannot agree, you can apply to the court for:

(a) an order that the custody of the child or children should be given to you, or
(b) an order that you are entitled to share with the child's mother all the 'parental rights and duties' in relation to that child. This means that the mother would have the actual day-to-day care of the child, but you would be involved in the upbringing of the child by jointly retaining rights and duties specified by the court – for example, where the child goes to school, or what religion he or she is brought up in;
(c) an order that you have access to the child.

If the mother of the child opposes your application, then the court may well order a welfare report to be prepared. In some areas, before a report is ordered, the court will require you and the mother to attend a conciliation appointment. This is an appointment with a court welfare officer to discuss the situation and to see whether there is any possibility of reaching agreement. If agreement is reached, then the court can be asked to make an order accordingly and, subject to being satisfied about the arrangements, will normally do so. If no agreement can be reached, the case will be adjourned for a welfare report to be prepared, and sometimes an order will be made giving temporary or interim custody to one of you until a final order can be made.

Court welfare officers in different areas have different ways of preparing reports, but they will always want to see you both and sometimes the children also, and some will continue to conciliate – that is, to encourage and promote agreement between you. The report will then be written and copies made available to you and the mother. If you are both prepared to accept any recommendation made in the report, then the court can be asked to make an order. If either of you is not prepared to accept any recommendation, then there will be a court hearing at which you can call witnesses to give evidence on your behalf, and at which the court welfare officer can be required to give evidence. The court will then decide.

If you should subsequently disagree on a question affecting the child's welfare, you can apply to the court to resolve the problem.

3 What about maintenance?

Agreements

It is possible to enter into a written maintenance agreement for the children. If you have agreed who is to have day-to-day care of the child or children and can agree an amount of maintenance, a written agreement will be a record of that.

Such an agreement can be varied or revoked by the court provided it contains an acknowledgement of paternity.

Court orders

If you cannot agree, either of you can apply to the court for an order against the other for financial provision in respect of the child. Financial provision means:

(a) Periodical payments or 'maintenance' – that is, weekly or monthly payments until the child is 17, although it can be extended if he or she is continuing with education or training.
(b) A lump sum payment.
(c) A transfer or settlement of property for the benefit of the child.

The court will decide the amount of maintenance or lump sum taking into account your income and expenses; your needs and resources; the age of the child; and his or her needs and resources.

It is possible for either of you to apply to the court at any time for the amount to be increased or decreased, if there has been a change of circumstances.

You can apply for such an order; it is enforceable even if you are living together when the order is made or start living together after it is made. It will cease to have effect if you marry or live together for more than six months.

These court orders replace affiliation proceedings, which were abolished from 1 April 1989. There is no longer any time limit for the making of an application for financial provision, and there is no longer a bar on married women applying in respect of a child not of the marriage. If the man denies that he is the father of the child, then the court can order blood tests or DNA genetic fingerprinting tests to be carried out. This involves blood samples being taken from the mother and child and the alleged father. These samples are then analysed. Blood tests can prove that a man *cannot be* the father, but they cannot prove that he *is*. DNA tests can prove, with very much greater certainty, that a particular man is the father.

4 Declaration of parentage

The child can apply for a declaration that a particular person is or was (if deceased) his or her parent.

5 Change of name

If you have adopted your partner's name while you have been living together, you may decide to change it again if you separate. No formalities are necessary. If you changed your name by deed poll the first time, it is advisable to change it again by deed poll. A deed poll is a short document that can be drawn up by your solicitor, declaring your change of name. It is possible, though not essential, to enrol your deed poll at the Central Office of the Supreme Court. Alternatively, you may record your change of name by making a statutory declaration.

If the child of the relationship was given the father's surname, the mother may decide that she wants to change that name on separation. This can be done without any formality. If, however, you want some evidence of change of name, you can sign a deed poll on your child's behalf with or without the consent of the father. Again it is possible, though not essential, to enrol the deed poll at the Central Office of the Supreme Court.

Reminders

* Make sure ownership of property is clearly set out with no room for doubt
* Make sure that if you are giving up secure tenancy or a career, for example, that your rights are protected
* Make sure of agreement if you separate as to:
  - who buys who out and the time limit
  - ownership of contents
  - liability for family loans
  - joint accounts and other assets
  - maintenance for children
* Make sure if you do separate that you notify the gas, telephone and electricity authorities, and the council poll tax office in writing, that you have moved out
* Remember your continuing liability for any joint accounts or credit

---

SECTION FOUR:
What Happens if One of You Dies?

Introduction

This section deals with what happens if one of you dies. Like most people, you would probably rather not think about what would happen if you or your partner were to die. This is natural, but it is important that you do think about this, because the rules that apply if there is no will can cause major problems for the partner left behind and will, at best, result in uncertainty at an already distressing time. You can easily avoid this by making wills now, and thus giving yourselves peace of mind.

Of course, if your relationship changes or finishes, you can always alter your will again at that time. Also, you should remember that if you later get married, even to your present partner, your will is automatically revoked; you should then make another will.

ONE: What Is a Will?

A will is a document in which you say what is to happen after your death.

You can say who is to inherit your estate. Your estate is everything you own and the people who receive it are called 'your beneficiaries'. You can say who is to carry out the practical aspects of sorting out your affairs. Such people are called 'executors'. You should choose people who are dependable as your executors, and it is better not to choose someone who is much older than you are and who is therefore likely to die before you. You can appoint your partner. A person can still be executor even if he or she benefits under the will. You can appoint your solicitor if this would be helpful to you, perhaps jointly with your partner or with a member of your family.

You can also in your will appoint a guardian or guardians for your children in certain circumstances if they are under 18.

The will may contain a 'legacy' or 'legacies', which are gifts of specific items. For example, you might want to leave your jewellery to a particular relative or friend, or gifts of stated sums of money – for instance, £500 to your godchild. The will also says who you want to receive the residue of your estate; that is, everything that is left after all debts and expenses, including funeral expenses (and any legacies), have been paid. The residue may go to one person or be divided between more than one. This is for you to decide. It is also usual to say in the will what is to happen if the person to whom you leave the bulk of your estate has died before you, or a short time after you.

Whatever you decide you want your will to include, it is essential that you have it properly drawn up, preferably by your solicitor. Precise words are needed because the will will only take effect after your death, when you won't be around to say what you meant. If the wording used in the will is confusing or ambiguous, it may be necessary for the court to decide what the words mean. If, on the other hand, the wording used in the will is clear, it will be strictly followed even though your family may know that it was not what you wanted. In both these cases, the outcome may not be what you intended. If you are in any doubt, you should ask your solicitor for advice.

There are extremely strict rules about the signing of wills and the people who witness your signature and, if these are not followed, the will or parts of it may not be valid. (See Example J.) Your solicitor will make sure the legal requirements are carried out.

Example J

George and Isabel knew that because they were not married it was important that they make wills to protect the surviving partner. To save money, they bought wills forms from a local stationer. They knew it was important to set out in simple terms what they wanted, and not to use words or expressions they weren't familiar with. They each wrote out carefully that the other was to inherit everything on their death. They took the forms with them when they went to visit Pat and Jerry, so that they could ask them to witness the wills.

While George was signing his will, Pat went to the front door to pay the milkman so she didn't actually see him sign. After George's death, Isabel's solicitor had to tell her that the will was completely void because both witnesses had not been present in the room when George signed. George's estate did not pass automatically to Isabel, who faced a long court battle to establish her claim.

Once you have made a will, or a new will, you will need to check that any previous will has been destroyed. Also, if you wish, your solicitor will look after your will for you until it is needed, usually at no extra charge. It is a good idea to make sure your family or the persons appointed as your executors know that you have made a will, and where it is.

You can always make changes to your will later, either by making a new will or, if the changes are of a minor nature, by making a codicil. A codicil is an additional document that will be read with your will and that must comply with the same strict rules about signing and witnessing as your original will. The codicil should be kept with the will.

TWO: How Your Estate Is Dealt With

The procedure for dealing with your estate is broadly similar, whether or not you leave a will. If you have made a will you will have appointed your own executor or executors to deal with or administer your estate. If you have not made a will, one or more of the persons entitled to your estate under the Intestacy Rules (see Chapter 3 on p. 121) will be appointed as administrators.

Executors and administrators are sometimes called 'personal representatives'. Your personal representatives will normally instruct a solicitor to do most of the work involved in administering your estate.

Unless the estate you leave is small, your executors or administrators usually need proof of their authority before property can be sold or money withdrawn from, for example, a bank or building society. To obtain this authority, an application must be made to a probate registry for a grant of probate, if there is a will, or a grant of letters of administration, if there is no will (or there is a will, but no executors are named in it, or the executors named have died). The probate registry is an office of the court. The application is made in writing and accompanied by the will, if any. The grant is then issued, and at this stage your personal representatives can sell or cash in your assets, and collect in the money. Out of this money debts are paid first, including funeral expenses and any inheritance tax if you leave above a certain amount. Out of what is left, the legacies, if any, are paid, and the residue passed to those entitled. If any beneficiary is under 18, the money or property to which he or she is entitled will probably have to be held on trust by your personal representatives until the child reaches that age. You may have said in your will that a beneficiary should not inherit before the age of say 21 or 25 and, in that case, the personal representatives will continue to hold the money or property until the beneficiary reaches that age.

THREE: What if You Don't Leave a Will?

If you do not leave a will, you are said to die 'intestate'. In that case it does not matter to whom you wanted to leave your property, money and possessions, or what you may have said to others about who was to have what. There are rules, known as the 'Intestacy Rules', which say who is to inherit your estate. The rules are designed to cover everyone who dies without leaving a will, and they may work unfairly as your individual circumstances cannot be taken into account.

Who does inherit your estate will depend on what relatives survive you. The Intestacy Rules provide as follows:

If you are survived by a husband or wife and children	(i) Your husband or wife receives: (a) Your 'personal chattels', which are basically personal and household belongings, but not cash or items bought for business use or solely for investment. (b) The first £75,000 of your estate (this figure is updated from time to time).

(c) Then the remainder is divided in two; one half is invested and the interest, dividends or other income is paid to your husband or wife for his or her lifetime. After his or her death, this half goes to your children at that time.

(ii) Your children receive:

(a) The other half of the remainder in equal shares. If they are 18 or over or married, payment is made as soon as the estate has been dealt with. If not, it is held until that time.

(b) After the death of your husband or wife, the invested half in equal shares.

Note: If any of your children has died before you, his or her share of the estate will be divided between any of his or her children who survive you (on age 18 or prior marriage). The same applies if one of those children has died before you, leaving a child or children who survive you.

If you are survived by a husband or wife (but no children), parents, or brothers or sisters of the whole blood (i.e. full brothers or sisters)	(i) Your husband or wife receives: (a) All 'personal chattels'. (b) The first £125,000 of the estate. (c) Half the remainder outright. (ii) If one or both of your parents are still alive, they receive the other half of the remainder. If both parents die before you, your brothers and sisters receive this half at age 18 or prior marriage. See *Note* above. Similar rules apply if any of your brothers or sisters die before you.
If you are survived by your husband or wife, but no children, parents or brothers or sisters	Your husband or wife receives the whole of your estate.
If you are survived by children, but no husband or wife	Your children take your estate in equal shares (at age 18 or prior marriage). See *Note* above.
If you are not survived by husband, wife or children	(i) If you leave one or both parents, they will inherit the whole of your estate.

(ii) If you don't leave parents but do leave brothers and sisters, they will inherit your estate (at age 18 or prior marriage).

(iii) If you have any half brothers or sisters (i.e. you only have one parent in common), they will only inherit your estate if you do not have any full brothers or sisters.

(iv) If you have no parents, brothers or sisters, but you do have one or more grandparents alive when you die, they will inherit the whole of your estate.

(v) If you are not survived by any of the above, then your uncles and aunts will inherit your estate. (This does not include any who are uncles or aunts by marriage.)

(vi) If you have any uncles and aunts who were only half brothers or sisters of your parents, they will only inherit if you do not have any uncles or aunts who were full brothers and sisters of your parents.

In the groups (ii) and (iii) (brothers and sisters) and (v) and (vi) (uncles and aunts), similar rules to those given under *Note* on p. 122 apply.

If there are no relatives in any of the above groups, then your estate will go to the Crown or, if you lived in Lancashire or Cornwall, to the Duchy of Lancaster or Duchy of Cornwall respectively. This is extremely rare since most people have some relatives who will be entitled, even if it may take a lot of time and money to track them down. If the Crown does receive an estate, it will often make a discretionary payment to anyone close to or dependent on the person who has died.

As you will see, the Intestacy Rules do not make any provision for your partner as you are not related. You may feel that this is not fair on the partner left behind, particularly if you have been living together for some time. (See Example K.) If you both want to provide some security for each other, it is important that you both make wills.

Example K

Albert and Dora lived together for forty-one years. At first it wasn't possible for them to marry as Dora was already married to Frank (who got drunk after the Cup Final one year and, in the ensuing row, stormed out of Dora's life for ever). Later on, Dora heard that Frank had been killed, but by that time there didn't seem any point in getting married and, in any case, it would have been embarrassing as their friends and neighbours all believed them to be already married.

Neither of them thought of making wills.

When Albert became ill Dora realized how little protection she had (the house was in Albert's sole name), but it didn't seem right to mention it to Albert when he was so ill. Then Albert died and, because he didn't leave a will, his estate went to his nearest relative, his brother in New Zealand. It took the solicitor seventeen months to find the brother, and it was another year before the court awarded Dora the right to live in the house and a share of the estate.

Note: A Law Commission Report in 1989 recommended an alteration to the Intestacy Rules so that if there was a surviving spouse he or she would inherit the whole of the estate. This report is now being studied, but it is not known when or if it will be discussed by Parliament with a view to changing the law.

There are no plans to alter the Intestacy Rules to include cohabitees.

FOUR: How the Intestacy Rules Could Affect You

1 Do you have a husband or wife still living?

As you will see, your husband or wife will be entitled to the main part of your estate. This is so even if you have lived apart for many years, unless your divorce (or Decree of Judicial Separation) has been finalized. This is also the case even if your husband or wife is living with someone else. Also, as the person entitled to the estate, your husband or wife is likely to be appointed to deal with it. This means he or she will have the right to take the decisions – perhaps even about your funeral arrangements – and will also, of course, have the right to collect and go through all your assets and private papers. Problems can obviously arise if it is not entirely clear what was yours and what belongs to your partner.

2 Do you have children, but no husband or wife?

Your children will inherit your estate in equal shares, and if you have children from your former marriage or a previous relationship they will be entitled to share in your estate with any children from your present relationship. In other words, all your children will inherit equally. This could mean that your house would have to be sold so that part of the proceeds could be made available to children from a previous relationship living elsewhere. This could leave your partner and any children living with you without a roof over their heads. (See Example L.) If this is not what you want, make a will.

Example L

When Bernard and Alison started living together, they were in agreement that they should have children; even though Bernard already had a grown-up son, Vincent, from his previous marriage, he was thrilled when Victoria was born. Alison gave up work to look after the baby and the family settled into the converted farmhouse that Bernard had bought before they met. Bernard knew that his son was doing very well in his own business. They had had a chat and Vincent had agreed that Victoria should be entitled to all of Bernard's estate if he died. Bernard didn't think it was necessary to bother making a will. When Victoria was eight, Bernard suffered a massive heart attack and died. As he had not made a will, Alison was not automatically entitled to any part of the estate. This was divided equally between Vincent and Victoria. Although he still thought Victoria should have the estate, things were not going well for Vincent. His business was in difficulties and, in addition, he was going through a divorce. Both his creditors and his wife's solicitor were soon aware of the increased value of his assets as a result of his father's death. Vincent couldn't afford to give up his entitlement. The farmhouse was sold so that his share could be paid to him, and Alison and Victoria moved away from the village to a small fifth-floor flat in a nearby town.

If your children or some of them are under 18 when you die, it will be necessary for at least two people to apply for a grant to administer your estate on the children's behalf. It is worth noting that one of those two people will almost certainly be the surviving parent of the minor child or children. This could well be your former husband or wife or former partner. This means that he or she will have the right to collect, go through and dispose of all your assets, including houschold and personal items. If this is not what you want, make a will appointing your own executor(s) to carry out your wishes. You might want to appoint your partner as executor even if you would still want your children to inherit.

Note: Remember only your own children benefit from your estate if there is no will. Your partner's children will have no automatic right to a share. In the same way, your children cannot benefit from your partner's estate unless he or she makes a will.

3 Creditors

If there is no one able to administer your estate or they cannot be found within a reasonable time, anyone to whom you owe money may apply to the court to be appointed to deal with your estate. They must distribute any surplus after expenses and debts are paid to the relatives entitled to your estate.

4 What about joint property?

If your house is in your joint names as joint owners, then it will pass automatically to the surviving party if one of you dies. This is because, as explained earlier, property owned jointly in this way is not affected by what is contained in a will or by the Intestacy Rules. It belongs to the surviving owner without any further formality (but see Chapter 9 on p. 159).

FIVE: What Is Your Position After Your Partner's Death?

To start with, there will be quite a few practical matters to take care of. Your partner's family may not automatically accept that you are the right person to do things such as registering his or her death and making the funeral arrangements, particularly if you have not been living together very long. If you think there may be a problem, it would be as well to make sure you do discuss the funeral arrangements with your partner's family before taking any steps.

Unless you are an executor, if you make the arrangements you will be personally responsible to the funeral directors for payment of their bill. Normally, you would be entitled to repayment from the estate but, if there is a disagreement with your partner's family, you may have problems in being reimbursed.

It is a good idea for you both to think out in advance whether you have any particular wishes about cremation or burial. You may also want to think about the possibility of your organs being used for transplants after your death. Your wishes can be recorded in your will but, above all, make sure someone knows, because otherwise it may be too late.

You will already have been in touch with your partner's solicitor to check if there is a will and whether it contains any instructions about the funeral. After the funeral, those entitled to administer the estate will instruct the solicitors to begin the process of sorting out your partner's financial affairs. Many people think that there is a formal reading of the will in the presence of all interested parties. This is, nowadays, extremely unusual. It is more likely that beneficiaries will be notified individually of their entitlement by the executors or by the solicitors.

Once the most urgent practical matters have been taken care of, you will want to know how your partner's death affects you and your financial position, the most important aspect of which is the home.

I The home

Joint owners

If you were joint owners, then the house will pass to you automatically whether or not your partner made a will (but see Chapter 9 on p. 159).

Owners in common

If you were owners in common, then your partner's share will pass to the person(s) entitled under his or her will or, if there is no will, to those entitled to his or her estate under the Intestacy Rules.

If your partner has made a will and has left his or her share of the home to you, then you will become the owner of the whole property (but see Chapter 9 on p. 159).

What if your partner's share is left to someone else?

The person who inherits the other share is likely to be anxious to be able to convert that share into money. For this reason, you could find that it is necessary for the property to be sold and for you to move out. However, you may not have to sell the home if you have sufficient funds, or can obtain a mortgage, to buy the other person's share. Alternatively, if you were financially dependent on your partner and are advised to make a claim against the estate (see Chapter 9 on p. 159), then if you are successful in your claim the court may give you the right to go on living in the home even if it does not give you your partner's share.

If you have to sell, how soon would you have to move out?

Your partner may have said in his or her will that the sale is to be delayed for a specific period to give you time to find somewhere else to live. If not, you would be expected to move out as soon as is reasonable to enable the sale to go ahead. This is something for you to discuss with the owner of the other share with a view to agreeing a timetable. If you cannot agree or you do not move out, then the other person can apply to the court for an order that the property be sold. The court will look at all the circumstances and, if it does order a sale, it may at the same time say that the sale is to be delayed for a specific period, again to give you time to find somewhere else to live.

The home is in your sole name

If the home is in your sole name, your partner's death will not affect that unless:

(a) You have previously made a deed or declaration of trust saying that your partner was entitled to a share of the property; in which case, it will mean that you were either joint owners or owners in common and the above paragraphs will apply.

(b) Your partner provided some of the purchase price or contributed to the value of the property in some other way, such as extending or improving it. If you are the main beneficiary of your partner's will, this may not be a problem. If not, if others have a share in the estate, it may be necessary for the court to decide whether the estate includes a share of your home. You may have agreed with your partner that any contribution he or she made would not entitle him or her to any share of the property. You could still have a dispute on your hands, unless you have satisfactory evidence of the agreement. If you have not made such an agreement, the court may decide that your partner's estate is entitled to a share of the home, and it will then also have to decide the extent of that share. This may again be difficult if you have not recorded, for example in a living together agreement, how that share is to be calculated. If your partner's estate is given a share of the home, then you would have to buy out the other beneficiaries or sell, as above.

(c) The property or part of it originally belonged to your partner and he or she made a gift of it to you within six years before his or her death. In this case, if there is anyone entitled to make a claim against your partner's estate under the Inheritance (Provision for Family and Dependants) Act 1975 (see Chapter 9 on p. 159), the court may regard the property or your partner's share as part of his or her estate when deciding the claim.

(d) The value of your partner's estate is not enough to pay off all the debts and he or she had made a gift of the property, or part of it, before death. In this case, depending on the circumstances, and how long before death the gift was made, the people to whom your partner owed money may ask the court to set aside the gift, particularly if it was made with the intention of avoiding paying creditors.

The home was in your partner's sole name

(a) Your partner may have made a will leaving the property to you outright.

(b) If not, then it will go to the person(s) entitled under your partner's will or the Intestacy Rules, unless, as above:
(i) your partner has made a deed or declaration of trust, acknowledging you have a share;
(ii) you can prove you have made a financial contribution to the purchase or improvement of the property and it was your joint intention that this should entitle you to a share (see Example M);
(iii) you can make a successful claim under the Inheritance Act (see Chapter 8 on p. 155).

Example M

Elsie and Fred had lived together since Fred first came out of the Army twenty-five years ago. The home was in Elsie's name but over the years Fred had greatly improved it by building an extension, converting the loft, and building a carport. Unfortunately, Elsie died without leaving a will and her estate went to her sister. Fred and the sister had never got on, and Fred found that his home was up for sale in double-quick time. His solicitor told him he could probably claim part of the value because of the contribution he had made, but proving those contributions did not turn out to be very easy, particularly since some of them were more than twenty years ago. The case seemed to go on and on, and eventually Fred settled for a very small sum rather than continue the unequal struggle.

The person(s) entitled to the home is likely to be anxious for it to be sold. If you have sufficient funds or can obtain a mortgage, you may be able to negotiate to buy the property, should you so wish. However, the beneficiaries can insist on it being sold on the open market, although you would, of course, be entitled to make an offer like any other potential purchaser.

If there is a sale, how soon would you have to move out?
Your partner may have stated in his or her will that the sale is to be delayed for a specific period to give you time to find somewhere else to live.

If not, you would be expected to move out as soon as is reasonable to enable the sale to go ahead. This is something for you to agree with the owner if possible. If you cannot agree or you do not move out, the owner can apply to the court for an order stating that you must leave to enable the property to be sold or the owner to move in. The court will look at all the circumstances and may give you time to find somewhere to live.

(c) Your partner has made a will leaving part of the property or part of his or her estate to you. Unless the value of your share is at least as much as the value of the property, then it will probably have to be sold; but at least you will have a lump sum which may help you buy another home. In some circumstances, one or more of the points in (b) (i) (ii) and (iii) above may apply.

House insurance

Whatever the circumstances, you should check that your partner's death is notified to the insurance company which covers your house and contents, since it may affect the terms of the policy – particularly if your partner was an owner or joint owner.

2 The mortgage

Nowadays, most people have bought their home with the assistance of a mortgage or mortgages. Your partner, or both of you, may have had some form of life assurance which should pay off the balance outstanding on the mortgage at your partner's death.

Should you go on paying the mortgage? This will depend on various factors.

Joint mortgage

(a) If the mortgage-linked life policy pays on your partner's death, the mortgage should be cleared by the insurance company and there is no need to continue the mortgage payments, although you should confirm this with the building society or other lender.

(b) If there is some other type of insurance policy which is not directly linked to the mortgage but that pays on your partner's death, you should seek advice from the solicitor dealing with your partner's estate, or your own solicitor.

(c) If there is no insurance that pays on your partner's death, then you will be responsible to the building society or other lender for continuing the mortgage repayments. You may be able to obtain partial reimbursement from your partner's estate if someone else is entitled to a share of the property.

Mortgage in your partner's sole name

Unless the mortgage is paid off by a mortgage-linked insurance policy, it will be a debt of the estate. Whether or not you should continue paying the mortgage depends on who inherits your partner's estate. You should seek advice from the solicitor dealing with your partner's estate, or your own solicitor.

Mortgage in your sole name

This is unaffected by your partner's death, and you will have to continue paying. If the mortgage payments were previously made from a bank account in your partner's name or in your joint names, you will need to make new arrangements for payment or, if previously joint, check that the standing order will still continue.

3 Tenancies

Joint names

If the home was rented in your joint names, then there should be no problem and the tenancy will simply continue in your name. An exception is if the tenancy came with a job and is conditional on you both continuing in that employment.

In your partner's sole name

If the home is rented from the local authority, you may be able to take over the tenancy if you were living at the property and this was your only home. You must also be a 'member of your partner's family' and have lived with your partner as 'husband and wife' for the twelve months preceding his or her death. If there are competing claims from other members of your partner's family, it will be up to the local authority to decide who should take over the tenancy.

If it is privately rented, you may be able to take over the tenancy if you were a 'member of your partner's family' and you were living with him or her when he or she died and for a specified period before his or her death. Again, there may be others who comply with the conditions but, in this case, the county court will have to decide who is entitled to take over the tenancy.

You may be regarded as a member of the tenant's family if you were living together as 'husband and wife'. The court will more readily accept you as a family if there were children. If there were no children, the court will more readily accept you as a family if the applicant is the woman.

In your sole name

If the tenancy is in your sole name, then there should be no problem. Members of your partner's family should not normally be able to make any claim against your tenancy.

4 Accounts and investments

Accounts or investments in your partner's sole name will form part of his or her estate.

Accounts or investments in your joint names may well cause problems (unless they pass to you outright), unless it is very clear how contributions to the account or investment were made and what you both intended at the time. Joint accounts and investments may not automatically pass to you and you may find, for example, that the bank freezes the account until it is clear who is entitled to the money. This could be a disaster if the bank will not allow you to continue to draw on the account. (See Example N.)

Example N

Desmond and Celia always budgeted very carefully. They knew the time of the year when the big bills for house and car insurance, poll tax and car tax were due, and made sure there was enough in their joint bank account to pay these. When Desmond had an accident at work and was killed, Celia was horrified to find that the bank would no longer allow her to write cheques on the account until Desmond's estate was administered. Without this, the red notices soon started to appear and the threat of being summonsed on the electricity account was almost too much for Celia.

Joint does not necessarily mean 50/50, and you may therefore have to sort out with whoever is administering your partner's estate how the money is to be divided. How much you get will depend on how contributions to the account were made, and what you both intended at the time.

5 Household and personal items

The position is similar to the above. That is, items belonging to your partner go to his or her estate, while the position regarding joint items is uncertain. It can be quite difficult to establish who owns what items after one of you has died, as it depends on who paid for them originally and what you and your partner intended at that time. It can be even more difficult to establish who owns items that were gifts to both of you from family and friends. These problems will obviously not arise if your partner has made an outright gift of household and personal items to you in his or her will.

6 Items bought on credit

If an item has been bought on credit by your partner in his or her sole name before he or she dies, then the estate will be liable for repayment and not you. However, the item will belong to the estate.

If the credit was in your joint names, then it is more than likely that you will be liable to continue the payments for the full amount outstanding.

The position is similar where there is a hire-purchase agreement.

7 Debts and liabilities

Debts in your joint names will generally become your sole responsibility. You may well have insurance of some sort, particularly if a substantial sum was involved, which will pay off the amount owed. Alternatively, you may be able to claim half from your partner's estate.

Debts in your partner's name alone will be a liability of his or her estate and will be paid out of the estate. Even if there are insufficient assets in the estate to pay off all the debts for which your partner was liable, you will still not be responsible for paying them. The only problem that could arise would be if, as mentioned earlier, your partner had made gifts to you within a specified time or to avoid paying creditors. In some circumstances, the value of the gifts might be taken into account.

Funeral expenses

These are also a liability to be paid out of your partner's estate and, indeed, take priority over other payments. The funeral director, however, is entitled to expect the person who ordered the funeral to pay for it initially. So if you make the funeral arrangements, you may have to pay and then reclaim it from your partner's estate. This may not always be as simple as it sounds.

SIX: What Can You Do to Avoid Some of These Problems?

The short answer to this question is to ensure that your joint intentions are recorded.

1 A living together agreement and/or deed of trust

As we indicated above, difficulties may arise after your partner's death if it is not clear who owned what.

(a) If you had jointly owned property or joint bank or other accounts, the size of your respective shares may not be clear, and it could be very difficult for you to prove how much you are entitled to. As you will have seen, it will depend on being able to prove your contributions and the intentions of both of you at the time.

(b) Contents are always a knotty problem. There are not usually any documents showing who owns them, as there are with a house for example. Ownership is therefore difficult to prove. Even with a car, a registration document is not proof of ownership.

An easy way to get round these problems is to set out in advance in a living together agreement the size of each of your shares or how these shares are to be calculated. The agreement can also set out who owns the contents: you, your partner or both of you?

The home needs to be dealt with in a rather more formal way and, if necessary, your solicitor will draw up a document known as a deed or declaration of trust. This will set out the shares in which you own the property and will be placed with the deeds.

2 How wills can help

Making a will enables *you* to make many of the decisions about what happens if you die and, in particular:

(a) Appoint executor(s)

You can appoint the person(s) you want to deal with the formalities and carry out the terms of your will. As has already been said, this can be important to your partner who might otherwise find themselves in a difficult position at a time of great stress. Remember, you can always appoint your solicitor as executor if this would be helpful to you. The executor(s) will normally ask a solicitor to take care of everything in any case. This means that appointing your solicitor as executor will not usually cost your estate much, if any, more.

(b) Appoint guardian(s)

If you have children under 18, you may also wish to name the person(s) you will want to look after them after your death. The guardian appointed in a will is called a 'testamentary guardian'. He or she may or may not have actual day-to-day care of the children: this will depend on whether or not the other parent is still alive, and able and willing to look after them. If you would be happy for the other parent to look after them (or continue to look after them), you may feel that there is no need to appoint a testamentary guardian. Alternatively, you may want to make an appointment that would only take effect if the other parent died before your children were of age. You cannot exclude the rights of the surviving parent but, even if the children live with that parent, the guardian appointed by you in your will will have a right to look after your children's interests and be consulted about their upbringing. If there were a dispute which could not be sorted out by the parent and guardian, and one of them felt it was sufficiently important, either of them could apply to the court to resolve the matter.

Either parent can appoint a testamentary guardian in respect of children of a marriage or former marriage. So far as children born outside marriage are concerned, unless the father has a court order giving him custody, or care and control or parental rights and duties jointly with the mother (for more details, see Section 3, Chapter 5 on p. 106), he does not have any right to appoint a testamentary guardian. Only the mother has that right. So, if you and your partner have a family, the mother may wish to appoint the father as testamentary guardian in the event of her death, and you may both wish to agree who is to be appointed as a substitute should you both die before the children are 18.

(c) Protect your surviving partner

As you will have seen earlier in this section, if you do not make a will, your partner is completely unprotected. By making a will you can provide for your partner to inherit the whole of your estate, or the major part of it. Even if this is not what you want because, for example, you have children of a previous relationship or other obligations, you can still help your partner in the following ways:

(i) By leaving him or her all the household items. You could consider making an outright gift to your partner in your will of your share of furniture and household items. This would avoid problems and arguments between your partner and the beneficiaries of your will as to who owns what. It would also avoid your partner having to face the effort and expense of replacing essential items such as, perhaps, the cooker and the washing machine. Your partner may not be able to afford this and, in any case, would you want him or her to have to cope with such things at this time?

(ii) By leaving him or her the car. This may be important if you live in an area not well served by public transport, or if your partner has to cope with ferrying children about. If you were buying the car with a loan or on hire purchase, you will obviously have to state in the will how the debt is to be paid off.

(iii) By delaying the sale of the home. If you have decided not to leave the home, or your share of it, to your partner, perhaps because you want this to go to your children, you may still feel that it would be unfair to your partner to have to look for other accommodation and move to allow the house to be sold immediately after your death. You can state in your will that the sale is to be delayed for, say, twelve or eighteen months. This will give your partner time to make alternative arrangements. This is not as simple as it sounds. There may be tax implications and also decisions will have to be made about who is to be responsible for such things as payment of the mortgage, repairs, outgoings and insurance. You would need to discuss this fully with your solicitor in order to decide if it is appropriate.

(d) Observing your obligations

There may be a number of people for whom you feel you should make provision in your will. In addition to your partner, there may be children of your existing relationship or a previous relationship. There may also be children who, though not yours, have been brought up by you. There could be other relatives, friends or charities you would want to benefit. Making a will enables you to balance these various claims where possible, taking account of the likely size of your estate.

You know your family and circumstances better than anyone else. Making a will puts you in control and means you decide who should inherit your estate. If it is clear that you have tried in the will to be fair, this will go a long way towards helping avoid conflict and court battles after your death.

Remember, you can always change your will later if your circumstances change.

SEVEN: State Benefits, Pensions and Insurance

This chapter looks at state benefits, pensions and insurance. The death of one of you may lead to financial hardship for the other, particularly if it is the main wage earner who has died. If you were living with someone, you are more at risk than if you had been married. This is because you may receive nothing if your partner has not made a will, or has made a will before your relationship began that does not include you. Even if he or she has made a will, this may say that the estate has to be divided between you and your partner's family; for example, children of a previous relationship. It is therefore very important for you both to consider what the survivor's financial position would be if one of you were to die, and what steps you can take to make things easier.

1 State benefits

If your partner dies, you will revert to being treated as a single person for assessment of your entitlement to Income Support, Family Credit (after the end of the relevant period), Housing Benefit and One Parent Benefit. Child Benefit is unaffected, except that, if it was being paid to your partner, you will need to have payment transferred to your name if the children are remaining in your care.

2 State pensions

Even though the Department of Social Security may treat you as 'husband and wife' for some purposes, you will not be entitled to a Widow's Pension or Widowed Mother's Allowance if your partner dies.

If you were receiving a Widow's Pension or Widowed Mother's Allowance before you started living with your partner, and this was suspended while you were living together, you should tell the Department of Social Security as soon as possible so that payments may begin again.

Your deceased partner's National Insurance contribution record will not be taken into account in calculating your state retirement pension, as it would be if it were your husband who had died.

3 Company pensions

Many people these days are members of company pension schemes in connection with their employment. If your partner was a member of such a scheme, you will need to get in touch with the company personnel or pension department, who will advise you on the position. Much depends on the rules of the individual pension scheme. Usually, it will be up to the trustees of the pension scheme to decide what benefits are to be paid and to whom. Most schemes allow the employee to complete a nomination form naming the people to benefit. The trustees are not bound by this nomination, but are likely to carry out the employee's wishes unless there are good reasons not to; so it is important for you to find out from the company whether or not your partner has nominated you. The trustees may well want time to look at all the circumstances before reaching a decision. If your partner had other obligations such as children from a previous marriage or relationship, the trustees may decide to split a lump sum payment between several people. Many schemes also provide for payment of a pension, although this will not automatically be available if you and your partner were not married.

What can you do?

Should you be a member of a company pension scheme, you will see from the above that it is important to check what the position would be if you were to die. If you want to provide for your partner to benefit under the scheme, you should make sure you nominate him or her (if your particular scheme allows this), so that at least the trustees have a record of your wishes. The nomination you make can always be cancelled and a new one made if you later separate.

4 Private pensions

Your partner may have taken out a private pension plan before his or her death. You will need to check the terms of the policy, or contact your partner's insurance or financial adviser. The terms of private pension schemes vary widely as to the benefits payable on death, and as to who is entitled to receive these benefits.

What can you do?

If you are not already a member of a pension scheme, you might want to consider whether you can afford to, and should, take out a private pension plan.

5 Life assurance

There may be insurance policies that pay benefits on your partner's death. If so, you should contact the insurance company to find out who is entitled to receive payment. If there is a mortgage-linked policy, you should also contact the building society or other lender, as they will probably arrange to make the claim in order to pay off the mortgage.

What can you do?

One way of obtaining greater protection for the partner left behind is to make sure you have adequate life cover. You should certainly ensure that the mortgage and any substantial credit purchases or loans are covered by insurance, so that they are paid off if you die.

EIGHT: Can You Make a Claim Against Your Partner's Estate?

If you are not provided for or not fully provided for on your partner's death, or if there is a dispute about ownership of property and you cannot settle this by reaching agreement with the personal representatives, you may be able to make a claim against your partner's estate.

1 For a share of the home and other assets to which you contributed

Where there is no deed of trust setting out your respective shares in the home, then the ownership or the size of those shares may be uncertain. As explained earlier, if the home was in your partner's sole name, but as a result of your contributions you consider it belongs to both of you, you may be able to apply to the court for a declaration that you are entitled to a share. The same applies if the home was in your joint names but, as a result of your contributions, you consider that your share was larger than appears from the title deeds. You will need to be able to prove that you made the contributions you say you made, that these added to the actual value, and that you both intended that they would entitle you to a share, or a larger share, of the property. Bear in mind that it may be difficult for you to bring a successful claim. For one thing, your partner will not be there to confirm or deny what you say your intentions were. In addition, you will have to produce evidence of the contributions you say you made. Not everyone keeps such precise records.

The above may also apply to other assets such as bank and building society accounts and investments.

To obtain a declaration from the court saying what the size of your share is, if any, will almost certainly take a considerable amount of time and can cost a lot of money. Having gathered together as much information as possible, you or your solicitor will need to set out in writing full details of your claim and your contributions. All the documents are then submitted to the court with the appropriate court fee. Copies would be served on your partner's personal representative(s), who would almost certainly file a defence with the court. After disclosure of all the relevant documentary evidence, there would be a court hearing that you would have to attend. The court would make an order saying whether or not you have a share and, if so, how much. The court would also give instructions as to how your share is to be paid or transferred to you from the estate. If you lose, the court could order you to pay the estate's legal expenses.

You may qualify for legal aid to help you take your case to court, but you may have to pay back your legal expenses to the Legal Aid Fund out of any money received at the end of the case or when the property is sold.

It is possible, if you win, that the estate may be ordered to pay some of your legal expenses.

2 Under the Inheritance (Provision for Family and Dependants) Act 1975 – commonly referred to as the 'Inheritance Act'

As the name implies, the purpose of the Act is to enable an application to be made to the court for terms of a will or the effect of the Intestacy Rules to be altered.

Not everyone can apply – only certain members of the deceased's family:

(a) husband or wife;
(b) former husband or wife who has not remarried;
(c) the deceased's children;
(d) in relation to an existing or former marriage, a child treated by the deceased as a child of that family.

In addition, you can apply if, immediately before your partner's death, you were living with him or her and were financially dependent on him or her.

If you feel that you satisfy these conditions, it will be up to you to prove to the court your claim that your partner supported you financially. You may have to produce detailed evidence of the financial arrangements between you and your partner; that is, who paid what. The procedure for making an application to the court is similar to that outlined earlier.

Again, bear in mind that such an application will almost certainly be opposed by the people entitled to your partner's estate.

What you would have to show

You will not be regarded as a member of your partner's family for the purposes of the Act simply because you were living together as 'husband and wife'. You will only be able to make a successful claim, therefore, if you can demonstrate that, immediately before his or her death, your partner was supporting you financially. This does not have to be total support. It may be enough to show that you are worse off financially than you were before his or her death and that, taking everything into account, it is reasonable that you should be awarded part or a larger part of the estate.

What the court will look at

The court will consider all the circumstances, including:

(a) the length of time you had lived together;
(b) your partner's other financial obligations, such as a previous family;
(c) the amount available in the estate;
(d) if there is a will, how long ago this was made;
(e) your own financial circumstances.

What the court will award

If you are successful, the court will order that you are to receive part or all of the estate, but will try to put you in the same position as you were in before your partner's death. This may not always be possible; the estate may not be large enough or may have to be divided between several people.

Remember also that the award is to compensate you for loss of financial support, and will not necessarily reflect the size of the estate left by your partner if this is large.

What about your children?

If they are also your partner's children, they can make a claim in their own right. If they are under 18, you can claim on their behalf. This claim would be separate from any you might make. There is one difference, though, in that, as children of your partner, they would not necessarily have to establish financial dependence and this would not be the only criterion in any award made by the court.

If your children are not also the children of your partner, they may still be able to claim (or you claim on their behalf), but they would need to show that they had been treated as 'a child of the family' and/or that they had been maintained wholly or in part by your partner.

Note 1: There are strict time limits for making a claim under the Act, so if you think this is going to be necessary you should contact a solicitor as soon as possible after your partner's death.

Note 2: The solicitor dealing with your partner's estate will be acting for the executors or your partner's relatives. Although he or she will usually try to be helpful to you, you should bear in mind that his or her first obligation is to the estate. For this reason, the solicitor is likely to advise you to consult another solicitor in order to have independent legal advice.

Note 3: The Law Commission which reported on the Intestacy Rules (see earlier) also recommended making cohabitees a special category of claimant under the Inheritance Act. This would make it easier to claim, as it would not rely on being able to show actual financial dependence. Again, it is not certain if or when this change of law will take place.

NINE:
Can Others Make a Claim Against Your Partner's Estate?

Apart from you and your children, there may be others who can claim under the Inheritance Act. This right cannot be excluded by will or by lifetime agreement. (It may, however, be excluded as part of a divorce settlement; so if your partner is divorced, he or she should check thc decree or order to be sure of the position.) So, even if your partner has made a will or you own the property jointly, there may be, for example, a claim from a spouse, ex-spouse or children. A claim can be made by a spouse, ex-spouse or children without having to show actual financial dependence on the deceased. If your partner was still married, his or her spouse may be awarded the sort of share that might have been transferred on divorce.

What the court will look at

In addition to the points outlined in Chapter 8 on p. 156, the court is also entitled to take account of:

(a) your partner's share of any jointly owned assets;
(b) any gift made by him or her within six years of death.

What can you do?

Remember, although these problems cannot always easily be solved, you and your partner can take positive steps by making wills that will set out your wishes and which may help avoid conflict later on.

Reminders

* Make sure your partner's family know and agree to you arranging the funeral, etc.
* Make a will:
  – dealing with outright gift of contents/car
  – possibly providing for sale of property to be delayed
  – which will be as fair as possible and help to avoid an Inheritance Act claim
* Make sure you have mortgage protection insurance
* Make sure any large debts are covered by insurance
* Check your company pension nomination
* Consider if you should arrange a private pension plan

SECTION FIVE:
What Happens if You Marry?

You might decide after living together for a while that you want to get married. You might always have intended to marry as soon as you were both free to do so or, perhaps, when you were ready to have children.

The effects of getting married

1 As soon as you marry you become subject to the laws of the land relating to married couples.

2 If the marriage fails:

(a) If the marriage then fails the court can, in certain circumstances, order one of you to pay the other maintenance.

(b) The court can also decide on dividing up the property, contents and other assets as it thinks fit. It will not only take account of what your intentions were when you bought, and what your financial contributions were. It will not even be bound by whose name is on the title deeds nor by what you may have said in a deed of trust.

It will decide what is fair, taking account of all sorts of circumstances that would not be relevant in a dispute between an unmarried couple, and it has the power to adjust shares accordingly. The court can also award you a share of property or business assets in your partner's sole name, which it could not do if you were not married.

When considering what order to make, the court would take account of a deed of trust made by you while unmarried, particularly if you both had legal advice when it was made. It will be evidence of what you intended, but you cannot override the authority of the court.

3 Any will you have made before marrying would be automatically revoked, so you would each need to make new wills. Even if you did not do this, the law makes special provision for your spouse to inherit your property or part of it.

Although your spouse would be entitled to inherit a part of your estate under the Intestacy Rules, and might even be able to claim a greater share under the Inheritance (Provision for Family and Dependants) Act (see Section 4), it is obviously much better for you to make another will immediately, because then your spouse will receive what you want him or her to receive rather than what the law or the courts state that he or she should receive.

4 Any children of your relationship would become legitimated. The birth could be re-registered. The father would then have equal parental rights with the mother. Whether a child is legitimate may be of rather less effect in the future than has been the case in the past, because of the desire of Parliament that laws should not refer to whether parents of children are or are not married. Illegitimate children now have exactly the same rights to maintenance, property, claims for compensation, benefits, etc. as they would have if born legitimate.

Marriage contracts

You can enter into a marriage contract. This can deal with many of the matters you can deal with in a living together agreement – such as who will pay the mortgage, the bills, and so on. However, you cannot override the authority of the court; so if you separate or divorce and cannot agree what should happen, the court will take account of the agreement, but will also take account of the other factors referred to above.

SECTION SIX:
Some Useful Definitions

You

Partner	This is what we have decided to call you in this book if you are living together, whether as 'husband and wife' or in any other financial or personal relationship.
Cohabitee	This is what you are likely to be called by official and semi-official organizations, for example the Department of Social Security. It usually only refers to you if you are living together as 'husband and wife'.
'Common law' husband/wife	There is no longer any such thing in English law (see Section 1), and this is therefore extremely misleading. It is, however, a term still in widespread use.

Meaningful live-in associate	This is what you may be called if you visit the United States of America.
Umm-er	This is what you are probably called by family and friends (as in, 'You've met my sister Rachel. This is David, her .... umm-er').

The Home

Title deeds ('deeds')	The documents showing the name(s) of the legal owner(s).
Registered title	In many parts of the country the legal ownership is 'registered' at the Land Registry.
Joint owners	You both own the whole property, are (almost always) entitled to equal shares if sold, and if one of you dies the other automatically becomes the sole owner. For historical reasons, this is usually referred to in legal documents as 'joint tenants'.

Owners in common: You each own a separate share of the property and, if it is sold, are entitled to the proceeds in these proportions. You can each leave your share under your will and (whether or not there is a will) your share will belong after your death to whoever inherits your estate. For historical reasons, this is usually referred to in legal documents as 'tenants in common'.

Severing the joint tenancy: If you are joint owners it is possible to change this to owners in common either by one of you serving written notice on the other or, if you both agree, by both of you signing a memorandum. You cannot alter a joint tenancy by will.

Declaration of trust: A document setting out what share of the property you are each entitled to. It is usually needed if the title deeds are in only one name; or in both names, but your shares are not clear.

Mortgage	The way most of us buy our homes, by borrowing the money from a building society, bank or other lending institution. You repay the loan over an extended period (25–30 years) or when you sell the house. The building society or bank protects itself by taking the legal right to sell the house if things go wrong and you can't continue the payments.
Mortgage protection policy	A simple form of life assurance that pays off the mortgage if you, or one of you, dies. If the mortgage is paid off during your lifetime, the policy lapses.
Endowment policy	A life policy which also operates as a form of savings/investment. You may receive payment after a number of years as it is not limited to payment on death.
Endowment mortgage	A type of mortgage that combines a mortgage of the home with life policy investment. You need independent financial advice as to what is best for you.

Deposit	A lump sum payment made by you as part of the purchase price. It is usually the difference between the price of the house and the amount of mortgage you can obtain.
Net proceeds of sale	The amount left after you sell the property and repay the mortgage, pay estate agency fees, legal costs and any other expenses of sale.
Equity	This is the term used to describe that part of the value of the house which is left after taking account of the amount of any mortgages outstanding. For example, if you own a house worth £80,000 and have a mortgage of £58,000, the 'equity' is approximately £22,000 since this is what you would get after sale, or against which you could take out further borrowing.

Credit

Bank loan	Usually a fixed amount with agreed monthly repayments over a set period, e.g. 24 months.
Overdraft	The bank agrees to let you pay more out of your account than you have in it. There will be an upper limit and, although there are no fixed repayments, the bank will expect you to pay off or at least reduce the overdraft within a fairly short period.
Hire purchase	A way of buying large items – such as washing machines – by instalments. Strictly, you hire the item to start with and only become the owner when the final payments are made. If you don't pay, the item can, depending on circumstances, be repossessed by the seller.
Credit sale agreement	Also a way of buying large items by instalments, but in this case you buy it immediately. Again, you may lose the item if you don't continue the payments,

	depending on how many payments have been made.
Credit cards	Provide continuing credit with (fairly) flexible repayments. The outstanding debt is not related to any particular item bought.
Credit cards (authorized user)	Many credit card institutions allow you to have an extra card for an 'authorized user', who can then make purchases using your credit. The original cardholder remains solely liable to the credit card company for the repayments.
Joint and several liability	If you take out any form of credit or loan in your joint names, then your liability will almost certainly be 'joint and several'. This means that the bank or credit company can enforce repayment of the whole amount due from either one of you, and not just your half share.

Wills and things

Will	A document, properly signed and witnessed, that sets out what is to happen after your death – who is to deal with administering your estate, and who is to inherit what you leave.
Codicil	Additional document, again properly signed and witnessed, which alters or amends your will. It is useful if the alterations are small. Otherwise, it is better to make a new will.
Estate	General term covering the sum total of what you leave when you die. Until the administration is completed and the assets transferred to the beneficiaries, your 'estate' is treated as a separate legal entity.
Administer	To administer an estate means to do all that is necessary to carry out the transfer to the beneficiaries. It includes complying with the formalities to obtain a grant of representation, collect in

	the assets, pay liabilities, and carry out the terms of the will or the intestacy provisions.
Grant	A grant of probate (if there is a will) or letters of administration (if there is no will or there is no effective appointment of executors in the will) is a document issued by the court to prove the authority of the person administering your estate.
Executor	Person appointed by will to administer your estate.
Administrator	Person appointed to administer your estate if you don't leave a will.
Personal representative	General term for either executor or administrator.
Testator	You – the person who makes a will.
Intestate	Dying without leaving a valid will.

Intestacy Rules	These say who is to inherit your estate if you die intestate.
Beneficiary	General term for anyone who inherits (benefits) from your will or under the Intestacy Rules.
Legacy	A gift under a will: can be a 'specific legacy' – that is, a particular item, or a 'pecuniary legacy' – that is, a fixed sum of money.
Residue	That part of your estate (usually the largest part) left after all debts, expenses and legacies have been paid.
Testamentary guardian	A person appointed by you in your will as guardian of your child or children if they are under 18 when you die. He or she will have joint responsibility with the surviving parent or any guardian appointed by that parent. Whether you appoint a guardian by will depends on your family circumstances, and whether it is appropriate.

Registration of death	By law, all deaths must be registered within five days of the death (or the death being discovered), normally at the register office for the district or sub-district within which the person has died. The doctor who certifies the death will usually have details of the person or persons who should do this. This sometimes depends on whether there needs to be a post mortem and/or inquest.

Taxation

Income Tax	Tax paid on the amount of income you receive. The percentage of tax payable is set in the Budget each year.
Personal allowance	The amount of income you can have before you start to pay income tax.
Mortgage tax relief	Provided your mortgage fulfils the conditions, you will get tax relief on the amount of interest you pay.

Capital Gains Tax	Tax payable on the increase in value of an asset or investment you own. Your house is exempt provided it is your main residence.
Inheritance Tax	Paid on the value of your estate when you die if you leave over a certain amount. There are certain exemptions available. There is also the possibility of Inheritance Tax on lifetime transfers in certain circumstances.
Community Charge ('poll tax')	This is a local tax that replaced general local authority rates for private households from April 1990. Each individual is liable for his or her own poll tax payments.

Some divorce terms

Divorce	The process of legally bringing a marriage to an end.
Decree nisi	An order made by the court when the divorce has almost gone through. There is then a

delay before the divorce becomes final. *You are not divorced if you only have a decree nisi.* You cannot remarry and your estate may go, if you don't leave a will, to your husband or wife.

Decree absolute — This is the order that makes your divorce final.

Judicial separation — Enables the court to make the same type of arrangements about the division of property and money and about the children as on divorce. However, you still remain married. Usually only people whose religious beliefs do not allow them to divorce apply for a decree of judicial separation, or those who have been married for less than a year and so can't yet get a divorce.

Maintenance — Court order (or agreement) on divorce or judicial separation, whereby one party makes regular payments (weekly or monthly) for the maintenance of the ex-spouse and/or children.

Lump sum order	Court order whereby one party makes a lump sum payment for the benefit of the ex-spouse and/or children.
Property order	Court order whereby one party transfers property, or his or her share of it, to the ex-spouse or children. Alternatively, the order may specify exactly when the property should be sold.
'Palimony'	Maintenance payments under United States divorce law is frequently called alimony. 'Palimony' is a slang word coined to cover applications by unmarried partners on separation. There is no such thing under English law.

APPENDIX ONE:
Living Together in Scotland

The law in Scotland is different in many respects from the law in England and Wales. This Appendix, dealing with living together in Scotland, covers the *major differences* and should be read in conjunction with the main part of the book.

The relevant sections are referred to in the Appendix by the same headings and paragraph numbers as are used in the main text.

SECTION ONE:
You, Your Partner and the Law

Introduction

'Common law' marriages

You may be held to be married by cohabitation with habit and repute in Scotland if you have lived there with the person for a few years, and were generally regarded as married by your friends, relatives and neighbours throughout that period. You must have both been free to marry. You need not have lived together in Scotland all the time, but a substantial part of your life together must have been there. You will have to go to court to have your marriage declared valid if others refuse to accept it.

You must have had the reputation of a married couple. People must have regarded you as married, not simply treated you in the same way as they would treat a married couple. Most couples who cohabit nowadays make no secret of the fact that they are not married. This means that they can never become married by cohabitation with habit and repute.

A person who is married by cohabitation with habit and repute has exactly the same rights and duties as any other married person.

Rights in the home

In Scotland, you are not the owner of the house unless your name is on the title deeds, or there is some later document granting ownership to you.

Right to provision on death

If you are not married to your partner, you have no claim to your partner's property on his or her death unless the will so specifies. You cannot apply to the court for a share.

Differences between marriage and living together

In Scotland, you will also commit incest if you have sexual intercourse with your uncle/aunt, nephew/niece, grandfather/grandmother, grandson/granddaughter, adoptive parent or adopted child. Intercourse with a step-parent or step-child is also a criminal offence if you are prohibited from marrying him or her – that is, if either of you is under 21 and/or the step-child has been part of the step-parent's household as a child.

A husband can be charged with raping his wife, even though they are not separated.

SECTION TWO: Living Together

One: Your Home

1 Buying

Your name must be on the title deeds in order to be regarded as an owner. The law takes no account of contributions, financial or otherwise, made by you as a non-owner. Your contributions are assumed to be gifts to the owner or made by you for your own benefit. You may be able to claim repayment of your financial contributions, but even this is very difficult.

In Scotland, if both names are on the title deeds, you and your partner are owners in common or co-owners. You own a half-share each unless the deeds specify different shares. When the home is sold, you and your partner will each receive your share of the proceeds.

Either of you can insist on the home being sold unless you have entered into an agreement not to do so. If you are a co-owner, you can state in your will who is to inherit your share of the home when you die. If you don't, your share will be dealt with according to the rules that apply when no will is made (the Intestacy Rules).

If you and your partner wish to own the home in such a way that each of you will automatically inherit the other's share, you can include in the title deeds what is called a survivorship destination. The property is described as belonging to you both (in whatever shares you wish) and to the survivor of you. If both of you helped buy the home, neither of you can leave your share by will to anyone else unless you both agree, and fresh title deeds are prepared without the survivorship destination or a written agreement is signed. If only one of you paid for the home, that person can leave his or her share to someone else, but the other cannot, unless you both agree and, as above, fresh title deeds are prepared or a written agreement signed.

Making mortgage repayments does not count as helping to buy the home.

If you want your contributions to result in a share or an increased share of the home, you must either have the title deeds changed or enter into a written agreement with your partner.

2 Renting

If your partner is the sole tenant of the home, you can apply to the court for the right to live there.

Two: Contents and Money

Items you buy using joint money belong to you.

When you buy a car with your partner's money it is yours, unless you bought it on his or her behalf. Your partner is entitled to demand that you repay the money.

Shares and other assets where there is a title certificate are different. Ownership depends on what the certificate says. The owners mentioned may later sign another document altering the ownership.

You are jointly and separately liable with your partner for your unpaid community charges due for the period that you lived together. As soon as you split up you should notify the Community Charge Registration Officer of this fact.

Five: Previous Relationships

Your Scottish court order for aliment will not provide that the amount payable ceases if you cohabit. Your spouse may, however, apply to the courts for the order to be reduced or cancelled. Your aliment will be reduced if you are being supported financially by your new partner, but not otherwise. It is up to you to show that you are not being supported. The position regarding periodical allowance payable after divorce is roughly the same. It ceases automatically if you remarry.

Lump sum and transfer of property orders will not be varied if you set up with a new partner after divorce.

Orders granting you occupation of the jointly owned home are rare in Scotland.

Six: You and Your Children

Parental rights cannot be the subject of an agreement in Scotland.

Under the Law Reform (Parent and Child) (Scotland) Act 1986, the father may apply to the court for any parental rights (custody, guardianship, access, etc.) to be exercised jointly with the mother. If full parental rights are granted, then the father and mother have equal rights. These rights are the same as those that a married coupled have in respect of their children. Parental rights cannot be assigned by an agreement.

Parents have only limited rights over a girl aged 12 or over and a boy aged 14 or over. Up to age 12 (girls) and 14 (boys), the parents act for the children in all litigation and carry out all property and other legal transactions on behalf of the child. After these ages, the children act themselves, but still need the consent of their parents. Some acts – like getting married, getting a job or making a will – don't require any parental consent.

You only have twenty-one days in which to register a birth.

The father's details can be entered on the birth certificate at the joint request of the mother and father if both go along to the register office, or at the request of one provided he or she has a declaration in a prescribed form by him or her as to who is the father of the child and a statutory declaration by the other confirming this. The mother can register a man as father on production of a decree of paternity.

The father's name can be entered later, on application by the mother; by the father, with the consent of the mother, or if he is a guardian or has custody; or by the child if aged 16 or over. Paternity has to be established by a court decree or declarations by both parents.

The name of a child under 16 can be changed with the consent of both parents, if alive. Scottish divorce decrees do not contain any provisions about changes of names. An 'unmarried father' is not counted as a parent unless he has been appointed as a guardian or awarded custody either solely or jointly with the mother.

In the case of a child aged between 16 and 18, the child applies to register a change of his or her own name. A parent's or guardian's consent is required.

SECTION THREE:
What Happens if You Separate?

One: Your Home

1 If you own your home

If you and your partner own the home together, each of you can normally insist on it being sold. But the court will not order a sale if you and your partner have entered into an agreement that the home should be sold only in certain circumstances and these circumstances have not occurred. Apart from this, a sale will always be ordered, whether or not you have children. For this reason, the terms of your agreement should be very carefully considered and legal advice sought.

Once your partner withdraws permission for you to live in the home, he or she can eject you without going to court. However, you can apply to the court under the Matrimonial Homes (Family Protection) (Scotland) Act 1981 for an order granting you the right to occupy your partner's home and an order excluding him or her.

2 How much will you get out of the home?

The shares you and your partner receive of the proceeds depend entirely on what the title deeds or any subsequent agreement say. If they say nothing about the shares, you get half each.

There is no room for argument about your share if the title deeds do not mention it, or there is no later written agreement dealing with the shares. You get half each, irrespective of your intentions or later contributions.

You will not get a share of the proceeds because you made financial contributions, unless this was agreed in writing. You may, if you are very lucky, get back the money you paid for the improvements even if there was no written agreement that you should. You may take items that you paid for which can be removed without damaging the home (fitted carpets and curtains, for example), as they remain your property.

Two: Contents and Money

In Scotland, anything you buy with joint money belongs to you unless you are clearly buying it on behalf of your partner. In that case, it belongs to your partner.

In the case of capital assets having a certificate of title – shares, for example – ownership depends on the name(s) on the certificate. This rule does not apply to bank or building society accounts. In these cases, ownership depends on whose money was put in and what you and your partner's intentions were.

Three: Maintenance

In Scotland, a person who accepts a child as a child of his or her family becomes liable for its maintenance. Acceptance requires at least a few years' support as part of the family.

Four: Violence

In Scotland, all criminal proceedings are brought by the Procurator Fiscal, a state official. The police will report any incident to the Fiscal, who then decides whether or not to bring proceedings. Private prosecutions are not allowed, except in very exceptional circumstances.

Interdicts

You can get a court order called an interdict prohibiting your partner from assaulting, threatening or molesting you. You do not need to combine this with any other proceedings. The court will grant an interdict fairly readily, especially if you can show that you have been ill-treated before. As soon as you have lodged your application in court, you can apply for an interim interdict. This is generally granted at once, without notice to your partner, and it gives you immediate protection. An interim interdict lasts until your application for interdict is heard.

There is a special kind of interdict called a matrimonial interdict. Despite its name, it is also available to cohabiting partners. To get a matrimonial interdict, you must either own the home with your partner or have been granted occupancy rights in it. You can apply for occupancy rights at the same time as you apply for interdict. You cannot apply for a matrimonial interdict if you are the sole owner or tenant of the home. The main benefit of a matrimonial interdict is that the court may attach a power of arrest to it. The police can then arrest your partner if they reasonably believe that he or she has done what the interdict prohibits. Your partner must be given notice of your application for a power of arrest to be attached.

Excluding your partner

If you are the sole owner or tenant of the home, you can simply ask your partner to leave. If he or she refuses, you can eject him or her or change the locks. You do not need to go to court.

If you and your partner own or rent your home together or your partner is the sole owner or tenant, you will have to apply to the court for an exclusion order under the Matrimonial Homes (Family Protection) (Scotland) Act 1981. To obtain an exclusion order, you will have to show that the order is necessary for your protection (or your children's protection) from conduct or threatened conduct which injures or is likely to injure the physical or mental health of you or your children. Even if you satisfy this test, the court will look at all the circumstances of the case to see whether exclusion is reasonable.

Your partner would almost certainly oppose your application for an exclusion order. This means that it will take some weeks before the court hears it. In the meantime, you can apply for an interim exclusion order, but your partner must be given at least seven days' notice of your application. The court applies the same tests as it applies in deciding whether or not to grant an exclusion order.

When granting an exclusion order, the court will also grant an order for your partner to be evicted from the home and an interdict with attached power of arrest prohibiting his or her return.

Five: Children

2 What does the law say about custody and access?

A father can apply to the court under the Law Reform (Parent and Child) (Scotland) Act 1986 to be granted all or some of the parental rights (custody, guardianship, access, etc.). He may apply for sole rights or rights to be exercised jointly with the mother. There is no Court Welfare Officer in Scotland. An independent solicitor is usually asked to investigate the case and report back to the court.

3 What about maintenance?

Your partner may enter into a written agreement to provide aliment for the children. Scottish agreements usually contain a clause enabling them to be enforced without going to court by registering them in the Books of Council and Sessions, so that you can arrest your partner's bank account or earnings or have his or her goods sold. The court can vary an agreement that it considers not to be fair and reasonable when it was entered into, and can vary the amount payable if the circumstances change later.

The parents of a child are jointly liable for aliment for the child. A court order for aliment takes the form of periodical payments until the child reaches the age of 18. It can be extended to age 25 if the child is receiving further education or training. Lump sums and settlements of property are not available, but the court can order small additional payments to meet 'one-off' extra expenses.

A court order for the child's aliment remains effective whether or not you and your partner live together again at a later date. But your partner could go back to the court for the order to be reduced or cancelled because support is already being provided at home.

5 Change of name

The mother may apply for registration of the child's name without the father's consent, unless he has been appointed guardian or has custody. Children aged 16 or over apply themselves.

SECTION FOUR: What Happens if One of You Dies?

In Scotland, your will is not automatically revoked if you later marry.

Example J on p. 117 would not apply in Scotland. The two witnesses need not be present at the same time.

Two: How Your Estate is Dealt With

The person(s) entitled to administer your estate on intestacy are called executor(s)-dative.

Executors (whether appointed by your will or the court if you leave no will) have to have their authority confirmed by the sheriff before they can administer the estate. To obtain this authority, they apply to the sheriff court for confirmation. The application form requires the executors to list all the assets of the estate, together with their individual values. Any will is sent together with a form. After a week or so, confirmation is granted and the will returned. If Inheritance Tax is payable, it must be paid before confirmation is granted. The confirmation application form is sent to the Capital Taxes Office in Edinburgh, together with the money. The receipted form is returned to the executors who then send it to the sheriff court.

Three: What if you Don't Leave a Will?

The Intestacy Rules are different in Scotland and provide as follows:–

If you are survived by a husband or wife and children

(i) Your husband or wife receives:

(a) The household contents up to a value of £12,000.

(b) A home which you own if he or she is living in it when you die up to a net value of £65,000. If the net value of the home is more, he or she gets £65,000 in cash.

(c) A cash sum of £21,000.

(d) One third of the remainder of your moveable property (property other than land or buildings).

(ii) The remainder of your estate is divided between your children. Descendants of a child who dies before you take the share the child would have taken had he or she survived.

Note: Children are entitled to their share whatever age they are. Money for young children is usually paid to their parents or guardians to invest on their behalf until they reach 18.

If you are survived by a husband or wife (but no descendants), parents or brothers or sisters of the whole blood (i.e. full brothers or sisters)

(i) Your husband or wife receives:

(a) The household contents up to a value of £12,000.

(b) A home which you own if he or she is living in it when you die up to a net value of £65,000. If the net value of the home is more, he or she gets £65,000 in cash.

(c) A cash sum of £35,000.

(d) One half of the remainder of your moveable property (property other than land or buildings).

(ii) The remainder of your estate goes to brothers and sisters and/or their descendants and your parents in

	accordance with complex rules. Half brothers and sisters inherit only if there are no full brothers or sisters or descendants of them.
If you are survived by your husband or wife but no descendants, parents or brothers or sisters or their descendants	Your husband or wife receives the whole of your estate.
If you are survived by children but no husband or wife	Your estate goes to your children. Descendants of a child who dies before you take the share the child would have taken had he or she survived.
If you are not survived by husband or wife or descendants	Your brothers, sisters, and/or their descendants and your parents share in accordance with complex rules. Half brothers and sisters inherit only if there are no full brothers or sisters or descendants of them.

If you do not leave any of the above relatives then your estate goes to grandparents, then uncles and aunts or their descendants (cousins, etc.) then great grandparents then great uncles and great aunts or their descendants (second cousins, etc.) and so on until some relative is found.

A cohabiting partner will not inherit under the Intestacy Rules, unless he or she can establish a marriage by cohabitation with habit and repute. In Example K on p. 125, a Scottish court would probably declare Albert and Dora to have been married in this way.

Four: How the Intestacy Rules Could Affect You

4 What about joint property?

If you and your partner own property in common with a survivorship destination in the title deeds, it passes automatically to the survivor if one of you dies.

Five: What Is Your Position After Your Partner's Death?

1 The home

In the absence of a survivorship destination, your partner's share passes to the person named in his or her will or, if there is no will, according to the Intestacy Rules.

You cannot claim against the estate, even if you were financially dependent. The court will always order the property to be sold if the person who inherits the other share insists.

Your partner's contributions to property held in your sole name will not give his or her estate any share in your property.

Gifts your partner made to you cannot be claimed back.

Your contributions will not give you a share, nor can you make a claim.

3 Tenancies

You are entitled to take over your partner's tenancy of a local authority house. The position is normally the same for a house rented from a private landlord.

Six: What Can You Do to Avoid Some of These Problems?

2 How wills can help

A father's appointment of a testamentary guardian is valid only if he was a guardian of the child when he died.

You cannot completely prevent your husband or wife or children from sharing in your estate. Whatever your will says, your husband or wife is entitled to claim one-third of your moveable estate (estate other than land or buildings). This fraction increases to one-half if you leave no descendants. Your children can likewise claim one-third or one-half if you leave no husband or wife. These rights, called legal rights, are automatic and fixed. They are claimed from the executors and no court proceedings are necessary. If you leave your husband, wife, or children something in your will, they have to choose between the legacy and legal rights. They cannot have both.

Eight: Can you Make a Claim Against Your Partner's Estate?

You will not be able to claim a share of the home as a result of any contributions you have made. You are unlikely even to be able to claim repayment of any financial contributions. The same rules apply to shares and other property with a certificate of title. On the other hand, you should be able to claim a share of a bank or building society account in the name of your partner if you put money in without the intention of making a gift of it to your partner.

The Inheritance (Provision for Family and Dependants) Act 1975 does not apply to Scotland. As a cohabiting partner you have no rights to your partner's estate if you are omitted from your partner's will, or he or she dies without a will.

Your children, if they are also your partner's children, would, however, be able to claim legal rights. These amount to one-third of your partner's moveable estate (estate other than land and buildings) if he or she also left a husband or wife, or one-half if there was no surviving spouse. The one-third or one-half share is divided equally among all your partner's children. You can claim on behalf of any children aged under 18 born to you and your partner. Legal rights are fixed fractions, but are due automatically. You do not have to go to court; you simply submit a claim to your partner's executors.

Although you have twenty years in which to claim legal rights, you should claim promptly, otherwise the executors may have paid away the estate to the beneficiaries.

Nine: Can Others Make a Claim Against Your Partner's Estate?

Your partner's husband or wife and children can claim legal rights out of his or her estate. They may claim these rights even if your partner leaves all the estate to you. If your partner leaves them something, they have to choose between their legal rights and what the will gives them. They cannot have both.

Your partner's husband or wife and children can renounce their legal rights while your partner is alive. They may not be willing to do so, however, without something in return.

An ex-husband or ex-wife of your partner cannot claim legal rights, but a separated spouse can.

SECTION FIVE:
What Happens if You Marry?

Wills made while you lived together are not revoked by your later marriage. You should look at your wills again and decide whether they still set out your wishes now that you are married.

APPENDIX TWO: Living Together in the Republic of Ireland

The law in the Republic of Ireland is different in many respects from the law in England and Wales. This Appendix, dealing with living together in the Republic of Ireland, covers the *major differences* and should be read in conjunction with the main part of the book.

The relevant sections are referred to in the Appendix by the same headings and paragraph numbers as are used in the main text.

SECTION ONE:
You, Your Partner and the Law

Introduction

Who lives together?

In Ireland there is a constitutional ban on the introduction of any law providing for divorce. Inevitably, therefore, many who suffer marriage failure and separate from their spouses form second relationships that cannot acquire the legal status of a marriage.

Attempts by Irish people to obtain foreign divorces do not solve this problem, as such divorces will only be recognized in Ireland if one of the spouses was *domiciled* in the country where the divorce was obtained. The Judicial Separation and Family Law Reform Act 1989 provides a broad range of circumstances in which a judicial separation will be granted, and gives the court wide powers to make property, financial and other arrangements on separation. The legislation is quite comprehensive, and is not unlike the provisions applying in England and Wales except that, on obtaining such a decree of separation, there is no right to remarry. Inevitably, therefore, second relationships are ones of cohabitation.

SECTION TWO: Living Together

Four: Does Living Together Affect Your State Benefits?

The state benefits are very different in Ireland, and you should consult the Department of Social Welfare or obtain a copy of the book entitled *Guide to Social Welfare Services*.

Cohabitation with another as 'husband and wife' will disqualify you (during the period of cohabitation) from entitlement to a Deserted Wife's Benefit or Allowance, a Widow's Contributory or Non-Contributory Pension, or the Unmarried Mother's Allowance. If cohabitation ceases, you may re-apply for the allowance/benefit, but you should expect a rigorous examination of the circumstances to satisfy the authorities that the new position is genuine. The Social Welfare Act 1989, once implemented by a ministerial order, will abolish many of these payments and provide instead for a Lone Parent's Allowance. However, cohabitation will still be a bar to a claim.

Note that the term 'adult dependant' for social welfare purposes only extends to spouses, not partners. However, each adult is entitled to their own social welfare payments if they meet the necessary criteria. This may prove difficult for a woman with a young child/children who is cohabiting. She will not be able to claim the allowances stated above and, if she is not available for work, she could not even claim unemployment benefit.

Five: Previous Relationships

Living with another may affect the maintenance you receive from your spouse for yourself, but not for the children. If the payment is made by court order, your adultery may be a reason for the court to decide that you should not receive maintenance for yourself. If you are being financially supported by another, this can also be taken into account. If the payment is being made under a deed of separation, you should check the terms of the agreement because they often contain a provision that maintenance of the spouse will cease in the event of cohabitation with another as 'man and wife'.

Your right to continue to reside in the family home may be subject to review in the event of cohabitation. Even if this matter is not dealt with specifically in your court order or deed of separation, it does constitute a change of circumstances and your spouse may seek a review of the arrangements. Your spouse may make an application to the court for an order for sale of the property.

Six: You and Your Children

The Status of Children Act 1987 abolishes all legal discrimination against children born to parents who are not married to each other. However, the provisions do not give automatic guardianship rights to someone who is the father of a child, but who is not lawfully married to the mother.

Provision has been made for a simplified procedure to enable such a father to apply to the court to become guardian – if he is registered as father on the birth certificate and if the mother consents in writing.

If the mother does not consent, the father can still apply to become a guardian. The court will decide if it is appropriate, taking into account that the welfare of the child is the paramount consideration.

A mother cannot by deed confer guardianship on the father, but the court can do so. She may, however, appoint the father or another acting in loco parentis as testamentary guardian of her child/children by will.

3 Registration of birth

Complications can arise on registration because of the old common law rule that all children born to a married woman are presumed to be the children of her husband. The registrar of births now adopts the following procedure:

Where a child is born to a married couple living together, the birth will be automatically registered with details obtained from the mother at the hospital.

In other cases, it will be necessary for the mother to register the birth herself. The biological father can be registered as father if any of the following are produced:

(a) Consent in writing of the husband of the mother.
(b) A separation decree from the court or a deed of separation dated at least ten months prior to the birth.

(c) A court order of paternity confirming who is the biological father of the child.

Seven: Does Living Together Affect How You Are Taxed?

I Income Tax

People living together are not entitled to married persons' tax allowances or tax bands. If both partners are working, they will both be entitled to their own personal allowances. However, if one is supporting the other, they must do so on a single person's net wage – which is often very difficult. It is possible to enter into a legally binding covenant (of not less than seven years) with your partner to pay an annual sum to them that is taxed relieved by the payer and not subject to income tax in the hands of the recipient if it is below their personal tax allowance level. A special income tax allowance for single parents will be lost in the event of cohabitation.

3 Gift Inheritance Tax

There is no gift or inheritance tax between lawful spouses. However, cohabitees are considered legal strangers for Capital Acquisitions (Gift or Inheritance) Tax purposes. The threshold level between strangers is only IR£10,400 and, since 2 June 1982, all gifts or inheritances from anyone else are aggregated. Therefore, even a modest gift/inheritance from your partner could give rise to a gift/inheritance tax problem. A series of gifts – such as the annual covenant referred to above – will be aggregated, and so the threshold level for gift tax can be used up very quickly.

There is no Stamp Duty on deeds transferring property between spouses, but there is between partners. Stamp Duty can range from 2 per cent to 6 per cent, with the highest rate being reached on values over IR£60,000.

Example:

Your partner wishes to transfer his house into your joint names. It is valued at IR£70,000.

Gift Tax

Value of gift passing		£35,000.00
Threshold		£10,400.00
Taxable on		£24,600.00
£10,000 @ 20% =	£2,000.00	
£14,600 @ 30% =	£4,380.00	
Total tax due	£6,380.00	

Stamp Duty

Value of gift passing	£35,000.00
Stamp Duty payable @ rate of 4% =	£ 1,400.00

The whole exercise will cost your partner £7,780.00

SECTION THREE:
What Happens if you Separate?

One: Your Home

In the absence of an agreement by joint owners to sell their property and realise their interests, application must be made pursuant to the Partition Acts 1868/1876 in order to divide or partition the property, or for an order for sale of the property in lieu of partition. This would result in each joint owner acquiring the vested entire interest in one-half of the original property as partitioned, or in one-half of the net proceeds of sale.

Partition, by its very nature, means a severing of the joint tenancy, but it can be followed by a physical division of the property; for example, dividing the property so that one joint tenant takes field A and the other joint tenant takes field B. In most applications for sale in lieu of partition, evidence is given by an auctioneer or some other qualified person that the property cannot be physically divided and partitioned – for example, as in the case of a semi-detached house. This is a necessary prerequisite for an order for sale in lieu of partition.

An order for sale in lieu of partition will not be made where the court sees 'good reason to the contrary' (Section 2, 1868 Act).

If such an application is being made by a husband or wife,

the courts will look at the criteria set out in the Family Home Protection Act 1976. This Act provides that the court will examine the needs and resources of both spouses and what alternative accommodation is being offered, its suitability, security of tenure, etc. There is no case law on whether the same criteria would be used by the court if one partner seeks such an order for sale against another, but it is unlikely. There are no reported cases of what criteria the court would apply to a cohabitee seeking a sale against their partner. Other than to say that an order for sale is not automatic and the court has a discretion to refuse such an order, the position is unclear. Because marriage and the family based on marriage are given a special status in the Irish Constitution, it is unlikely that case law relating to similar applications between spouses would be followed for cohabitees, although it could be used as authority.

If you are not the legal owner of your home, you may be asked to leave by your partner without undue formality; and if you refuse to do so, an injunction can be granted by the court forcing you to do so. Conversely, if you are a legal owner you can ask your partner to leave and terminate his/her licence to stay.

Your partner may sell the house if he/she is the legal owner and your consent to such a sale is not required. A spouse in such a situation has the benefit of the Family Home Declaration Act 1976.

Three: Maintenance

Neither of you has a claim for maintenance against the other for yourself. If there are children of the relationship, you are entitled to seek support for them. If you are a woman, you may be entitled to apply for the Unmarried Mother's Allowance if you are no longer residing with your partner and are unmarried. If you are deserted by your partner, however, you are not entitled to Deserted Wife's Benefit or Allowance. If you were receiving this benefit or allowance before you started cohabiting, you can apply for it to be reinstated, but you can expect a rigorous examination of the circumstances to satisfy the authorities that the new position is genuine.

Four: Violence

A Barring Order (equivalent to an Ouster Order) may only be granted on the application of a spouse.

Where no marriage relationship exists, a civil injunction may be obtained restraining your partner from attending at or near your home, threatening you or using violence against you or your children, and any other order that the court may consider appropriate. Such injunctions are usually granted in cases of emergency, and are unlikely to be continued indefinitely to deprive your partner of his or her legal rights in relation to the property.

Five: Children

An unmarried mother is the sole guardian of her child but, as we have already seen, the biological father can apply for guardianship. The father can also apply under the Guardianship of Infants Act 1964 for custody and access to his child. The court considers all cases on the basis that the welfare of the child is the first and paramount consideration. The court will examine the relationship that the child has had with the father in the past, and whether his relationship with the mother was permanent or casual.

The father of the child in such cases may voluntarily enter into a written agreement for the maintenance of the child or children or, failing agreement, the court may make a periodical payments order. A father can agree to make a lump sum settlement instead of periodical payments, but the court does not have power to make such an order if the father does not agree.

Maintenance is payable for children until the age of 21, provided the children are receiving full-time education or instruction at any university, college, school or other educational establishment. There is no upper age limit for maintenance and support of children suffering from mental or physical disability to such an extent that it is not reasonably possible for the child to maintain himself/herself fully.

SECTION FOUR:
What Happens if One of You Dies?

One: What is a Will?
Two: How Your Estate is Dealt With

It is very important, if you wish to protect your partner after your death, that you take legal advice and make a will making appropriate provision.

If you have been married, your spouse may have retained their rights to inherit as provided in the Succession Act 1965, even though you are no longer living together. Alternatively, both you and your spouse may have either by deed of separation or by order of the court renounced or had your Succession Act rights extinguished. If this is the case, then you are free to dispose of your property by will without reference to your spouse.

If such renunciation has not taken place, your spouse has a legal right share to inherit one-third of your estate if you die leaving a will. This legal right share may take precedence over the terms of your will if your spouse elects to take their legal entitlement.

Children have no automatic entitlement to any specific share in your estate. However, Section 117 of the Succession Act provides that if you do not make provision for your children as a 'just and prudent parent', the children can make an application to the court.

Children in this context means any biological child of the deceased, and the children do not have to be minors. You cease to be a minor at the age of 18 following the Age of Majority Act 1985. Some cases have recorded provision being made for 'children' in their thirties and older!

Three: What if You Don't Leave a Will?

The following are the Intestacy Rules that apply if you die without leaving a will, or where your will for one reason or another is invalid or incomplete:

If you are survived by a husband or wife and children	(i) Your husband or wife is entitled to receive two-thirds of your estate. (ii) And your children are entitled to the remaining one-third.
If you are survived by a husband or wife (but no children)	Your husband or wife receives your entire estate.
If you are survived by children, but no husband or wife (or husband or wife has renounced)	Your children take your entire estate in equal shares. *Note:* Children means all

	biological children, both marital and non-marital.
If you are not survived by husband, wife or children	If one or both of your parents are alive, they will inherit the whole of your estate.
If you do not leave any of the above or parents	It will be divided equally between your brothers and sisters and more remote relatives.

The Intestacy Rules do not make provision for a partner as you are not legally related, and it is therefore essential that a will in the proper format be drawn up by a solicitor acting on your instructions and having regard to all your circumstances.

Five: What Is Your Position After Your Partner's Death?

If a spouse within three years of the date of death divests himself/herself of assets with the intention of reducing the size of the estate available for distribution on death, such dispositions can be set aside by the court if, for example, the effect is to deprive the spouse and marital children of proper provision on death.

Because of the low threshold level of Inheritance Tax between legal strangers, the drafting of your will should take account of the possible tax implications of any gift. Your solicitor will be able to help.

Seven: State Benefits, Pensions and Insurance

You will not be entitled to a Widow's Pension on your partner's death. You may be entitled to some benefit from your partner's employers/company pension scheme, as many schemes can make a discretionary payment to a dependant who is not a spouse. The trustees of such schemes will take into account the wishes of the member if they have made their wishes clear during their lifetime by completing a nomination form or Letter of Wishes.

5 Life assurance

Depending on the circumstances of each case – for example, financial dependence – an insurance company can accept that you have an insurable interest in your partner and permit insurance policies to be taken out to cover, say, the amount due on the mortgage on your home or other debt. The proceeds of such a policy, if the premiums are not paid by the beneficiary, will constitute an inheritance and be subject to Capital Acquisitions Tax at the rates already mentioned.

Eight: Can You Make a Claim Against Your Partner's Estate?

If your partner has provided for you by will, but had made no provision for his/her legal spouse and/or children, the spouse, if they have not renounced their rights, can look for their legal right share and the children can seek a share of the estate from the court. If the applications are successful, it may erode the provision made by your partner in his or her will.

If your partner has not made proper provision for you or dies without leaving a will, you have no claim for any share in the estate. In Ireland, there are no similar provisions to those contained in the Inheritance (Provision for Family and Dependants) Act 1975, which applies in England and Wales. You are therefore limited to claiming a percentage interest in property or chattels that you have made a financial contribution towards acquiring, with all the difficulties of proof which that entails.

SECTION FIVE: What Happens if You Marry?

In Ireland, lawful marriage of cohabiting couples is limited to those who are single and unmarried, or have a validly recognized divorce, or a final decree of nullity (very rare). As there is no divorce available in Ireland, most cohabiting couples cannot lawfully marry as one or both are married to someone else.

Be warned that obtaining divorces in faraway places such as the Dominican Republic or Haiti and remarrying in equally exotic locations are rarely recognized as lawful marriages in Ireland, and you should proceed and take the precautions that are suggested herein for cohabiting partners.

Index

Note: References to Scottish and Irish law are on the whole not separately identified under main headings, since it is important that readers in these countries refer to the detailed discussion in the main body of the text, and not simply to the Appendices, which only cover *differences* from English law.